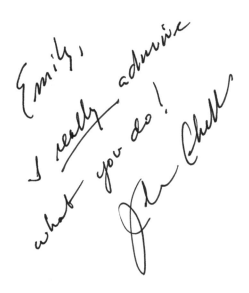

Emily,
I *really* admire
what you do!

John Chubb

Praise for *The Best Teachers in the World*

"John Chubb's *The Best Teachers in the World* thankfully rescues us, just in time, from the usual long list of qualities, skills, and degrees we should demand of our teachers. Instead, he looks closely at how great teachers are born in our best schools, places such as the Knowledge Is Power Program, in which educators are allowed to work together and create approaches that respond to real conditions in disadvantaged neighborhoods. More time, creativity, and leaders carefully trained to know what teachers need would give us far more great teachers than we have now. This should be required reading for all parents, all school boards, and, most particularly, all education schools."

—Jay Mathews, *Washington Post* education columnist and blogger, author of *Work Hard. Be Nice.: How Two Inspired Teachers Created the Most Promising Schools in America*

"This slender volume is a much-needed breath of fresh air. While education reformers dream up new ways to train, evaluate, and pay the same teachers for doing the same job the same way they always have, John Chubb dares to suggest a much more promising path to reforming the profession. He explains how technology can help change the nature of teacher work, how we might reduce the number of teachers in order to dramatically boost pay, and how school leaders can be empowered to value teachers for things beyond reading and math scores. Chubb's book is an essential read for educators, advocates, and policy makers frustrated by today's debates—and even more critical for those who haven't yet grasped the trouble with today's pinched debates."

—Frederick M. Hess, director of education policy studies at the American Enterprise Institute (and author of *Education Unbound*)

"Twenty years ago we all shared the intuition that teachers matter a lot. Now we have the science to prove it. What we don't have is either the social consensus or the compelling social science on how to use that information to improve student outcomes. The policy debate has been narrow and largely devoted to the value of value-added. John Chubb steps into this fray with a broader and bolder perspective, one that tries to harmonize what are typically discordant notes of education reform: technology, schools of education, choice and competition, leadership, assessment and accountability, class size, international benchmarking, and, yes, teacher value-added. *The Best Teachers in the World* is beautifully written, thoughtful, and provocative. It is up on the hillside rather than down in the weeds. I highly recommend it."

—Grover "Russ" Whitehurst, senior fellow and director of the Brown Center on Education Policy at the Brookings Institution

"John Chubb has it exactly right: US students will never have the great teaching they deserve unless we break away from the one-teacher-one-classroom model. If we don't, we're doomed. If we do, teachers can earn more—within budget. And vastly more students can have access to 'the best teachers in the world.'"

—Bryan C. Hassel, PhD, codirector of Public Impact

The
Best Teachers
in the World

EDUCATION
next
B O O K S

*The Hoover Institution and Education Next Books
gratefully acknowledge the following individuals
and foundations for their support of this research on
education policy and reform.*

LYNDE AND HARRY BRADLEY FOUNDATION

KORET FOUNDATION

EDMUND AND JEANNIK LITTLEFIELD FOUNDATION

THE BERNARD LEE SCHWARTZ FOUNDATION, INC.

TAD AND DIANNE TAUBE
    TAUBE FAMILY FOUNDATION

The Best Teachers in the World

Why we *don't* have them and how we could

Foreword by Benno C. Schmidt, Jr.

John E. Chubb

HOOVER INSTITUTION PRESS

STANFORD UNIVERSITY | STANFORD, CALIFORNIA

www.hoover.org

EDUCATION
next
B O O K S

An imprint of the Hoover Institution Press

Hoover Institution Press Publication No. 630

Hoover Institution at Leland Stanford Junior University,
Stanford, California 94305-6010

First printing 2012
18 17 16 15 14 13 12   7 6 5 4 3 2 1

Manufactured in the United States of America

The paper used in this publication meets the minimum Requirements of the American National Standard for Information Sciences—Permanence of Paper for Printed Library Materials, ANSI/NISO Z39.48-1992. ∞

Library of Congress Cataloging-in-Publication Data
Chubb, John E., author.
    The best teachers in the world : why we don't have them and how we could / John E. Chubb.
        pages cm. — (Hoover Institution Press publication ; no. 630)
    Includes bibliographical references and index.
    ISBN 978-0-8179-1564-3 (cloth : alk. paper) — ISBN 978-0-8179-1566-7 (e-book)
    1. Teacher effectiveness—United States.   2. Teachers—Selection and appointment—United States.   3. Teachers—Certification—United States.   4. Teachers—Training of—United States.   I. Title.
    LB2832.2.C48   2012
    371.1—dc23   2012028282

To Angela, a remarkable principal—and wife

Contents

CONTENTS

The Envy of the World

Benno C. Schmidt, Jr.

I have had the good fortune to lead some of the most prestigious institutions of higher education in the world. I served as dean of Columbia University's School of Law and as president of Yale University, two esteemed private institutions. For the last twelve years, I have been chairman of the board of trustees of The City University of New York (CUNY), the largest urban public university in the world. Columbia and Yale educate some of the highest achieving students in this nation. CUNY educates a far wider range of students, including large numbers of the economically disadvantaged, racial and ethnic minorities, recent immigrants, and first-generation college attendees. Each of these institutions also does an excellent job of educating the students it aims to serve.

I have also had the privilege to work with our nation's public elementary and secondary schools. I left the presidency of Yale to become CEO of The Edison Project, an ambitious private sector venture to introduce new and innovative school designs into public education. The company, which was later known as Edison Schools and today as EdisonLearning, went on to manage or support hundreds of public schools, for the most part in inner cities and impoverished communities where better school-ing is desperately needed. It was at Edison where I met and first worked with John Chubb. It was also where I came to under-stand how incredibly challenging the work of K–12 education is. There is nothing more important to this nation's future than public education, yet nothing more difficult.

The work of our public schools is also tougher than the job of higher education. Public education must meet the needs of *every* child in America. Higher education is needed by more and more Americans every year, particularly as our economy becomes more sophisticated. But the mandate of higher educa-tion is simply not as broad as that of our public schools. This is important to acknowledge—and from years of practical experi-ence, I absolutely do. At the same time, I believe higher educa-tion may have something to teach our public schools. Colleges and universities serve millions of students with economic and academic difficulties, CUNY being a major case in point. The work of higher education is also hard.

To its great credit, the United States has managed to develop a system of higher education that is widely regarded as the best in the world. According to the *Times of London*, seven of the top ten universities in the world are American. So too are eighteen of the top twenty-five and fifty-three of the top hundred. Nearly 1 million students worldwide now attend our colleges and uni-versities—the highest number of foreign students in the world. The system is not without its issues, about which more below. But, warts and all, our system of higher education is the envy of the world.

The same cannot be said of our system of elementary and sec-ondary education. Our K–12 schools, whatever one may believe their exact rank, are not regarded as the best in the world or even among the contenders. Most international comparisons of stu-dent achievement place the United States in the middle of the pack. How incongruous to lead the world in one domain and be an also-ran in the other.

But how fortunate to have a highly successful system, right at home, from which we might learn. In reading John Chubb's new book, I was struck repeatedly by the parallels to higher education. The title of the book itself resonated with my experience in the university world. "The *Best* Teachers in the World." Why not, I thought? The United States has the best colleges and universities in the world; why not the best schools, too? And if schools are to be the best, their teachers must be world-class as well. I thought especially of my experience at CUNY.

When Mayor Rudy Giuliani asked me to chair a task force on The City University of New York, I knew I was in trouble. The only two things I knew about CUNY were that it was big and that it was caught in a terrible spiral of decline. I told the mayor that I was the worst possible person he could choose; that I had spent my whole life in private universities—Yale and Columbia—that were completely different; that critics would say I knew nothing about public universities and would be right; that everyone at CUNY would view me as nothing more than a hatchet man. "That's why you're the right person for this," the mayor grinned. "I want a fresh look." You don't say no to your mayor.

Even so, CUNY is a special challenge. It has been "America's equal opportunity factory" (*The Economist*'s phrase, not mine) for New York's poor and immigrant communities for over 150 years. It serves 270,000 degree-seeking students, and an equal number in "adult education" programs. Its economic impact on New York City is hard to exaggerate. For example, today, CUNY accounts for 20 percent of all construction in New York City.

It took me a year to finish the task force report. I titled it *An Institution Adrift*. I fully expected that it would sit on the shelf and collect dust. I may even secretly have hoped for that, as my confidence that I knew what was right for CUNY lessened the more I learned. For better or worse, that was not to be. New York Governor George Pataki and the mayor called a press conference and announced that they were appointing Herman Badillo, the bravest person I have ever known in public life, as chairman and me as vice-chairman of the CUNY Board of Trustees. A couple of years later, when Badillo ran for mayor, I succeeded him. I'm still there.

Since I first got involved with CUNY in 1997, the institution has found its stride and has moved boldly forward. The number of full-time faculty has increased from about 5,500 to about 7,100. Student enrollment has gone from 200,000 to 270,000. The university serves more minority, poor, and immigrant students than ever. Annual giving has gone from $37 million to over $250 million. Most important, by measures both quantitative and qualitative, students are enjoying more success.

I share this story because it illustrates what educational institutions are capable of accomplishing—if they are willing to embrace major change. I am proud of what Columbia and Yale accomplished on my watch. But those institutions have enormous advantages that CUNY does not. CUNY transformed itself by systematically raising standards and then accepting the wrenching changes that higher standards entailed for students, faculty, and university leaders. There was lots of innovation, too—whatever it took to make CUNY the institution the city needed it to be.

Our public schools are a lot like CUNY. They face the challenge of educating large numbers of students for whom learning does not come easily. They are institutions with long-established practices, often protected by politics and therefore highly resistant to change. CUNY finally broke through these obstacles. It is possible, I believe, for public schools to do the same.

Doing so will require acceptance of reforms much bolder than public education has been willing to accept heretofore. Public schools would do well to look to higher education for ideas and inspiration. John Chubb begins his search for the best teachers by considering how technology might make teachers more effective. This is an idea so obvious it would go unnoticed were we talking about any industry other than K–12 schools. The history of economic progress—of increasing standards of living, generation after generation—is a story of innovation, usually rooted in technology. Inventions in one industry after another enabled fewer people to produce more and better products and services and to earn higher incomes in the process. People were also freed from laborious work in older industries to invent and develop new ones.

Higher education has been at the forefront of technological innovation in teaching and learning. Elite institutions like Stanford, Harvard, and MIT have launched multimillion-dollar projects to offer their courses for free to hundreds of thousands of students worldwide. Today, 25 percent of all college students take at least one course online. For-profit colleges have doubled their enrollments over the last decade, largely through online offerings, and are competing with traditional institutions for students. All of higher education is looking at technology as a way to halt steady tuition increases—hikes that are putting college out of reach for millions of families or burdening students with years and years of debt.

Higher education is also being driven by the measurement of quality—another reform that Chubb recommends. University presidents decry the many college rating systems, such as *U.S. News & World Report*. Ratings trivialize the complex value of a university education. They encourage institutions to "game" the ratings rather than engaging in real improvement—encouraging more applications in order to reduce acceptance rates, for example. But the ratings also shine a bright light on things that matter, like freshman retention rates and graduation rates. The federal government used the 2008 reauthorization of the Higher Education Act to require colleges and universities to be much more transparent about their performance statistics, so that students can make wiser decisions about where to enroll. The Obama administration has been pushing harder in this direction with its proposed new College Scorecard.

New discoveries in assessment make it now possible for colleges and universities to analyze how much value they are adding for students as they progress. Innovative institutions are using measures like the Collegiate Learning Assessment to do this.

Chubb recommends that public school teachers no longer be required to be certified through a university-based teacher training program or its equivalent. He urges experimentation in teacher training, with decisions about qualifications to be left to hiring school districts or charter schools. The only policy requirement is that training programs and institutions submit to formal evaluation of their effectiveness. With transparent indicators of performance, prospective teachers could make better decisions about where to seek training and employers could make better decisions about where they recruit their teachers.

The United States currently has 1,400 colleges and universities training teachers. Some surely do very good work; many surely do not. Currently, the good and the bad have the same authority to certify teachers. That makes little sense. Imagine if colleges and universities could not certify. They could offer degrees and training programs. But employers—school districts and charter schools—would be the sole arbiters of whether teachers' training prepared them to teach. Policymakers would aid employers by rating training programs based on the success of graduates in school classrooms—including raising student achievement. Colleges and universities would need to improve their performance—and ratings—or risk losing prospective teacher enrollments. The evidence is that higher education would respond.

Finally, Chubb recommends more attention to leadership. Better compensation (which technology could make possible) and better training (which could be promoted by measuring its success) should deepen the public school talent pool. But those measures are unlikely to be enough. In my experience, college and university faculty care as much about the non-material elements of their jobs as they do the material ones. They care about the culture of the department, program, school, or college in which they work. They care about the values of their institution. They care about the institution's regard for their scholarship and service. These qualities cannot be captured in formal work rules, though rules matter. They cannot be legislated or negotiated. In my experience, an important reason that U.S. universities tend to be superior internationally is that their practices are not rigidly prescribed by government authorities. The U.S. system provides wide berth for university presidents, provosts, deans, and other leaders to build faculties consistent with distinct missions and values.

The U.S. higher education system, of course, is not a government system. It is a mixture of public and private, not-for-profit and for-profit, institutions. It is a mixture of baccalaureate and doctoral institutions, of universities that emphasize research and colleges that exist to teach. The government subsidizes the system through grants to schools and aid to students. But all schools, public or private, compete for students. Like firms in any competitive market, all colleges and universities must innovate, adapt, or lose students and resources to their competitors. Since 1990, over a fourth of all private colleges have succumbed to the competitive pressure. Higher education, over the same period, has generally prospered. Enrollment is up by one-fourth and the stronger institutions have thrived.

Do not misunderstand my comments here as a paean to the market. My point is far more practical. American colleges and universities are often steeped in tradition and resistant to change. They have not adapted easily or without leaving problems unsolved. But compared to universities internationally, and compared to our system of K–12 education, American higher education is a dynamic system. Its dynamism has enabled it to embrace technology, to accommodate performance measures, and to empower leadership to make decisions while being held accountable.

Research in K–12 education has begun to provide statistical support for something I observed time and again in my public school experience. Principals make a huge difference for school performance. I never saw a great school without a strong principal. They worked their magic, I believe, by building effective teaching staffs. Chubb argues that policymakers should put much more faith—and responsibility—in school leaders. They may hold the key to teacher quality.

I would not presume to say whether this recommendation or any of the others in this book are correct. I am not an expert in K–12 education. What I will say with confidence is that the ideas in this book are already at work in America's colleges and universities, helping to drive change. America's higher education system is far from perfect. Our colleges and universities see far too many students matriculate without ever earning a degree. Achievement gaps rival those in K–12 education. Costs have grown too fast and for too long. But perfection is not the standard. U.S. higher education is still the best in the world. U.S. schools, too, could be the envy of the world—if we, as a nation, are willing to embrace some of the lessons that higher education has to teach.

PREFACE

This book is less a product than a byproduct. I have never conducted formal research on teacher quality or written previously on the subject. Some readers may say after reading this book that those shortcomings are obvious. But what I do bring to this effort is many years of practical experience recruiting, training, developing, and promoting teachers. From 1995 to 2009, I was Chief Education Officer of EdisonLearning, previously Edison Schools and The Edison Project, which I helped to found. During that time, I worked in literally hundreds of public schools, traditional and charter, in twenty-five states and the District of Columbia. Most of the schools served students who were economically and academically disadvantaged.

My experiences with teachers, principals, and schools led me to certain beliefs. Among the strongest: nothing influences student achievement more than the quality of the teachers, and nothing influences the quality of teachers more than the quality of the principals. In recent years, during my part-time career with the Koret Task Force, where I try to keep my formal research skills from dulling completely, I have followed with great interest the burgeoning econometric literature on teacher and principal effectiveness. I have been heartened to see my practical conclusions—shared by many practitioners, by the way—reinforced by rigorous analyses. I decided to write about both: the practice of teaching and the research behind what works.

I also decided it was time for me to write about teachers and technology. This topic also grew out of experiences at Edison. From the earliest days of that enterprise, Edison experimented with technology. We gave home computers to students and desktop models to teachers beginning in 1995, when the utility of these devices was still far from clear. We experimented with blended learning schools in 2005, when the term "blended learning" had not been invented. We launched full-time online learning in 2009, before that industry began the rapid climb it is on today. I have written about some of this experience before, in *Liberating Learning* with Terry M. Moe (San Francisco: Jossey-Bass, 2009). That book focused on the politics of technology. In recent years, the politics have slowly started to change, as we predicted, and schools are now experimenting with technology much more extensively and creatively than only a few years ago. Those experiments, coupled with my own experience, have led me to believe that teaching may finally be on the verge of important breakthroughs. I wrote this book, in part, to suggest what those might be.

I was also influenced to write by practical experiences after Edison. I had opportunity in 2010–2011 to spend time with many of the leading schools and colleges of education in the United States. I worked on a project for the Abu Dhabi Education Council in the United Arab Emirates—with my colleague, Benno C. Schmidt, Jr.—to bring a major U.S. school of education to Abu Dhabi. Benno and I visited a dozen of the highest ranking education schools in the country. In the end, Peabody College at Vanderbilt University showed the greatest interest, and we spent a year and a half working with the dean and faculty of the school as well as leaders of the university. As I came to understand better what Peabody does, I developed enormous respect for its training programs. I also had to challenge my own understanding of education schools. Research indicates very clearly that, on average, they do not benefit teachers. Yet, if the United States is to have better teachers, they must be better trained. Can policymakers learn something from the apparent successes of Peabody? Or is formal teacher training as hopeless as research suggests? I have tried here to reconcile the conflicting evidence.

Researchers and practitioners often talk past one another in the search for truth and solutions. I have tried here to be sensitive to the understandings of both. I have spent my career in both worlds, and—as a byproduct—I am regularly trying to square those experiences. I do believe we are at a pivotal moment in school reform, turning largely on the role of teachers. Policymakers now mostly agree that teachers are the key to higher achievement. They now have at their disposal powerful new tools, rooted in technology, which can accelerate improvements in teacher quality. With this book, I have tried to examine, from the perspective of research and practice, the levers that have the most potential to lift teacher quality to the levels this nation requires.

Because this book was so long in the making, I have many debts of gratitude. I emphasize, before acknowledging them, that none of the individuals or institutions that aided or inspired me share responsibility for the views I have taken from them. What I got right or wrong here is entirely my doing.

I begin with deepest thanks to the hundreds of principals and thousands of teachers with whom I worked at Edison Schools and EdisonLearning. Special thanks go to the charter boards of our schools in Dayton, Ohio, and West Covina, California, which allowed us to launch some of the first blended learning models in their schools. A shout-out goes to my friend, Anthony Kim, who taught me about online learning while he was CEO of Provost Systems and who introduced me to some compelling hybrid models—profiled in this book—in his current job as CEO of Education Elements, a new blended learning company.

Many people gave very generously of their time to be interviewed for this book. Three principals of schools implementing blended learning—Denise Patton, Mickie Tubbs, and Mike Kerr—were genuine inspirations. My friend and former colleague, Richard Barth, has been showing me what leadership looks like for many years. As CEO of KIPP, he spoke with me at length about that remarkable organization's leadership development program. Richard and his colleague, Steve Mancini, gave me access to everything I could have wanted to read about KIPP leadership programs.

At Peabody College, so many people were helpful I am afraid a thank-you list will omit somebody, so I will not try to write one. I single out a few critical participants, but appreciate the assistance of all. Dean Camilla Benbow was incredibly forthcoming, not only about what her program tries to do but about the issues that plague education schools more generally. I value her candor more than she likely knows. Professor Marcy Singer-Gabella not only provided many insights about Peabody and teacher education, she arranged every one of the dozen or so interviews that I conducted. I am grateful to all of the College leaders and faculty who spoke so openly with me about the challenges of teacher training and the criticisms that teacher colleges face. I also enjoyed immensely talking with current and recent Peabody students; America is lucky to have such lively minds entering our classrooms. I finally want to thank the leaders of Vanderbilt University—Chancellor Nicholas Zeppos, Provost Richard McCarty, and Vice Provost Tim McNamara—without whom my relationship with Peabody would never have begun. To all of my friends at Peabody and Vanderbilt, I hope I got your story right.

This book ultimately would never have been written without the support of my colleagues on the Koret Task Force on K–12 Education at the Hoover Institution at Stanford University. Throughout our nearly fifteen years together, in myriad projects joint and individual, there has been one constant: the demand for serious scholarship. We have never been a blog-happy crew, ready with opinions without thorough consideration of research or original investigations. My Koret colleagues have challenged me to test all of my ideas about teachers against the relevant scientific research. I hope now, after years of refinement, that the arguments I make here are stronger and better documented for all of the back-and-forth with the Task Force.

In the end, every member of the group—Bill Evers, Checker Finn, Eric Hanushek, Paul Hill, Caroline Hoxby, Tom Loveless, Terry Moe, Paul Peterson, Herb Walberg, and Russ Whitehurst—read and commented on the manuscript twice. I appreciate the considerable time and care that each put into the effort. I also thank the Hoover Press, its staff and editors, especially Barbara Egbert and Barbara Arellano. I am very grateful to The Koret Foundation and its president, Ted Taube, whose generous support has enabled our team of scholars to work together these many years and who directly supported the writing of this book. As with all things task force-related, Richard Sousa, senior associate director at Hoover, was very helpful in ushering this book through the writing and publishing process. Of course, none of this would have been possible without the leadership of Hoover Institution Director John Raisian, who launched the task force and has guided it through thick and thin.

John E. Chubb

CHAPTER 1

Wanting the Best

"My manicurist requires a license to do my nails, but our nation isn't sure we should license teachers."

Camilla Benbow, Peabody College

amilla Benbow is the dean of the top-ranked school of education in the United States, Peabody College at Vanderbilt University in Nashville, Tennessee. Under her leadership, which began in 1999, Peabody has risen in stature—passing Harvard, Stanford, and other elite institutions—to reach the top spot in the *U.S. News & World Report* rating system, which it has occupied since 2009.[1] Peabody is the only school of education in an elite national university that trains undergraduates to become licensed K–12 teachers.[2] Because Vanderbilt is a very selective institution overall (ranked in the top twenty of national universities), and because the brightest high school students in the United States have few choices if they wish to become teachers upon graduation from a four-year institution, Peabody enrolls extremely high-achieving students. Their average SAT combined math and critical reading score in 2011 was 1438.[3]

Benbow and Peabody have been doing precisely what many experts have argued in recent years must be done if U.S. schools are to produce students who can achieve with the very best in the world.[4] They are attracting the top students from America's high schools to become teachers. They are putting them through a clinical model of preparation requiring 800 hours of school-based experience, in addition to the rigorous academic requirements of a Vanderbilt bachelor's degree. It is well documented that high-achieving nations such as Finland, Singapore, and South Korea, among others, have selective teacher education programs that channel top-performing high school graduates into teacher preparation that balances demanding academic instruction with pedagogical training in schools.

But Benbow and Peabody are also part of an enterprise under siege. Schools of education have been the subject of withering criticism going back to the 1980s, when the United States first became alarmed about student achievement. This criticism has been intensifying in the last decade.[5] In 2006, Arthur Levine, then president of Columbia University's Teachers College, led a comprehensive study of U.S. schools of education that documented their failings in excruciating detail.[6] As a group, schools of education are non-selective. Their students post SAT scores at or below the average of all college graduates. Education school faculty members are weak in research and are dated in practical experience. The vast majority of U.S. teachers are produced in lower quality colleges and universities. The list goes on. In the last year, the National Council on Teacher Quality has begun publishing its findings on the attributes of teacher education programs, beginning with student teaching. The results of exhaustive research show teacher education programs failing to meet literally all standards—as Levine concluded five years before.[7]

Making matters worse for schools of education, sophisticated statistical analyses have been unable to find any benefit in teacher education for student achievement. Licensed or certified teachers appear to perform no better than teachers without certification or those certified through alternative routes.[8] The time required for traditional certification through a bachelor's or master's degree in education also deters many bright students from even considering teaching. Teach for America (TFA) has become the number one employment choice of Ivy League graduates—over one in ten apply—because it provides a route into teaching that requires only five weeks of summer training and no degree in education.[9] Smart young people want to teach; they just don't want to jump through needless hoops to do so. Research shows that TFA recruits perform at least as well as traditionally certified teachers.[10] Taking all of this into consideration, reformers are asking if teacher licensing is necessary at all.

But when Benbow asks if the nation is now ready to give up on licensing a profession that is infinitely more important and demanding than manicuring, she is raising a question that should concern us all—not just deans of schools of education. Of those elements that are within the control of schools, teachers are the most important determinant of how much students achieve.[11] Family and personal attributes of students have the greatest effect on achievement. But among the elements of *schooling* that promote performance, teachers have the most impact by far. Research offers varying estimates of the impact, but it is safe to say that several consecutive years with highly effective teachers—the best 20–25 percent—can move students quite a way in the national achievement distribution.[12]

Since the 1980s the United States has aimed to become the highest achieving nation in the world. Through Republican and Democratic presidential administrations, the nation has aspired to produce the kinds of students who can compete with any on the planet. In the internationally competitive knowledge economy, education is vital to productivity, growth, and standards of living. Teachers are mission-critical. If the United States is going to raise student achievement to the highest levels in the world, it will need to have the best teachers in the world. A recent and renowned analysis by the management consulting firm McKinsey & Company put it this way: "The quality of an education system cannot exceed the quality of its teachers."[13] Within school walls, nothing comes close to the importance of teachers.

So, if the United States is not to select, develop—and license— teachers through traditional means, how should it proceed? How *shall* the United States build the strongest teaching force in the world? Should the nation try to attract and keep significantly higher-aptitude students in teaching, as Peabody is doing? Should our best colleges and universities develop teacher preparation programs for undergraduates as well as graduates, as international leaders have done and, again, as Peabody is doing? The United States has the best system of higher education in the world. In the most recent *Times of London* rankings, seven of the top ten, eighteen of the top twenty-five, and fifty-three of the top one hundred universities were American.[14] Is it not possible that this great resource—especially the best institutions and the best students—might be used to enhance a profession as important as teaching? Or, given the success of alternate routes to teaching, such as TFA, should the United States abandon university-based certification and open teaching to anyone with a bachelor's degree who can prove himself or herself on the job?

Being Serious About Being Best

For all the talk among political leaders about being first in the world in math and science or otherwise having the best schools and highest achievement in the world, there is little talk about having the best teachers. Yet, research is increasingly clear that that is exactly what the aim of top achievement requires. If the United States wants the best achievement in the world, it will need to seek out, train, and retain the best teachers in the world. The United States is not currently serious about that aim.

Consider: the United States is now in the process of trying to establish high common academic standards for public school students. Over the last decade the states have set proficiency standards that vary widely in their expectations of students and that frequently fall short of standards set in the National Assessment of Educational Progress (NAEP), the "nation's report card" for the last forty years. Through the Common Core project most states are now working together to establish voluntary national standards with proficiency expectations closer to those set in NAEP. Today's teachers, however, do not come close to meeting the academic standards being set for students. A proficient score on NAEP reading or math translates into at least a 600 on the SAT, or about a 1200 overall.[15] The most generous estimate of the aptitude of new U.S. teachers recently estimated SAT scores of 515 in critical reading (formerly verbal) and 506 in math, or 1021 overall. But this estimate looked only at twenty states where the SAT is the dominant college entrance exam, and these states are higher achieving on average than other (ACT-dominant) states.[16] It may be possible for teachers to educate students to levels above their own accomplishments. But a 200-point gap between teacher performance and student expectations amounts to a world of difference.

U.S. education policy shows no serious intent to reduce this gap. The federal government's most important education policy, Title I of the Elementary and Secondary Education Act (ESEA), otherwise known as No Child Left Behind (NCLB), requires that states ensure all teachers are "highly qualified"—meaning state-certified and subject-matter competent. Most states have implemented these requirements by requiring new teachers to take Praxis I and II assessments (unless they have a relevant college major). But states frequently set Praxis passing scores at levels that translate into SAT reading-math scores of about 1000—well below current expectations for students.[17]

Once on the job, teachers are rarely held accountable for student achievement, even though their schools have been held to account since NCLB was adopted in 2002. The Obama administration is encouraging states to use student achievement as part of teacher evaluations, but the efforts are just beginning and achievement remains a relatively small part of the new systems. By international standards teachers are not highly compensated in the United States—at least one factor that determines the quality of individuals attracted to a profession and willing to stick with it.[18] The list goes on. U.S. education policy is not serious about high-quality teachers.

Attracting, developing, and retaining the best teachers in the world will require radically different policies and practices from what the United States currently follows. The United States is simply too far off course for anything else. Fortunately, there are lessons from school systems abroad and in the United States to provide guidance. There is substantial research about what affects student achievement, and what does not. There is also solid evidence of what helps teachers, and what does not. This book offers a new strategy for raising teacher quality to the highest levels in the world. It is based on scientific research. It is also based on prominent examples of schools, colleges, and other educational organizations actually doing things very differently.

Cases in Point

Peabody College at Vanderbilt University merits a close look. It is rated number one at what it does by its peers, excels by all objective measures, attracts the highest achieving undergraduate and graduate education students in the nation, employs some of the most distinguished figures in education research, and provides training along the lines of the most respected training institutions internationally—but already tailored to the United States. If education schools need ideas of how to improve teacher quality, Peabody would seem the most likely place to find them. Dean Benbow, her senior faculty and administrators, and numerous students were good enough to participate in interviews for this book, supplementing the public record.

Another obvious source of ideas is schools where students are achieving, especially with students who do not achieve easily themselves. The choice here is the Knowledge is Power Program (KIPP). Since 1994, KIPP has slowly built a network of charter schools in disadvantaged communities with documented success in raising student achievement. Its approach is simple: each school is built by an extraordinary principal whose job it is to recruit, develop, and retain high-quality teachers. For reasons now reinforced by research, this approach holds much promise for improving teacher quality. The CEO of the KIPP Foundation, Richard Barth, and key staff helped explain how KIPP prepares leaders and leaders prepare teachers. The U.S. Department of Education awarded a $50 million grant to KIPP this year to support replication of this approach in KIPP schools and select traditional public schools.

Efficient schools may prove as important as effective schools for boosting teacher quality. If teaching is to become an esteemed profession able to attract and retain the best and brightest, it will need to provide better compensation, recognition of performance, intellectual stimulation, opportunities for growth, and more. Teaching in U.S. schools today can be drudgery, only partly occupied with instruction, often filled with repetition, and compensated without regard to merit. In other industries, this sort of wage labor has been replaced by highly skilled and more professional roles, created through technological innovation.

U.S. schools are beginning to experiment with new mixes of teachers and technology, to benefit students and improve the job of teaching. Some schools are getting far more from a smaller number of teachers. Leaders at three such schools— one elementary, one K–8, and one high school, all in the Los Angeles area—were kind enough to share their stories and achievements with me.

A Different Strategy

These case studies enrich the research and bring to life a strategy for raising teacher quality that is very different from the approach this country has historically followed. It takes seriously the aim of raising student achievement to levels comparable to those of the best nations in the world. It therefore largely rejects the approach to teacher quality that has been this country's hallmark—but which has not given us the best teachers in the world. The new strategy has three major elements:

1. The United States will never have a world-class teaching force unless teaching attracts and retains higher caliber individuals. Teachers drawn on average from the lower ranks of high school graduates simply will not do. To attract higher potential teaching candidates and to retain the most successful of them, the teaching profession must become more attractive relative to alternative lines of employment. This means work that is less menial and more expert, less prescribed and more responsible. It means less wage labor and more pay for performance. It means substantially better compensation. It does not, however, need to mean more education spending. The United States already spends more on education per capita than most any nation in

the world. It should not need to spend more. The teaching profession can be improved by helping teachers be more productive. As in every industry before it, education can improve productivity by turning to technology. Reconfiguring schools to use teachers and technology to the best of their respective abilities could transform teaching. The profession would become more selective, requiring perhaps 20 percent fewer teachers overall. The work would become more differentiated and more highly skilled. Pay could be raised materially. These changes could reverse the brain-drain that has plagued teaching since women gained other opportunities more than a generation ago. Teaching could once again be a destination for top talent.

2. Teaching is not an art, to which some are born and others are not. It is an intellectually demanding endeavor that can and should be guided by research-based practice. Teachers should be trained, both before they take charge of a classroom and thereafter. They should not be trained, however, in the schools of education that predominate today. They should be trained in institutions and programs able to demonstrate their efficacy in producing teachers who raise student achievement. The last point is critical, as teacher quality has no meaning apart from student achievement. This training might well take place in universities and schools of education like Vanderbilt and Peabody, strong in research and practice. But it could also be provided by entities such as Teach for America, The New Teacher Project, or programs yet unknown—as long as they can demonstrate their efficacy in producing teachers who can help students learn.

3. School leadership is critical to quality teaching. Principals have major influences on teacher development on

the job, coaching teachers directly and helping teachers learn from one another or receive the external training they require. Principals play a lead role in creating the school culture that shapes student achievement. Principals create the working conditions that help determine whether great teachers remain. Principals evaluate teachers on all of the practices that go into student achievement, and should help schools keep the best teachers and improve or shed the weaker ones. Principals specifically must retain top quartile teachers, replace bottom quartile teachers, and hire new teachers with higher probabilities of success. High-quality teaching therefore requires a different approach to the hiring and training of school principals, one that focuses, in a word, on achievement. Candidates for the post of principal should offer hard evidence that they have helped students learn, and subsequent training should emphasize the same.

These three elements comprise an approach to teacher quality which is fundamentally different from the U.S. norm, which is grounded in licensing and credentialing. As odd as it may seem to license manicurists and not teachers, as Benbow points out, that is precisely what U.S. policymakers should do—or at least the not-licensing-teachers part of the comparison. The United States needs to attract as many high-caliber people into teaching as possible, and licensing requirements today serve largely as an impediment to attracting high quality. There is no evidence that licensing or certification creates better teachers or even sets a floor beneath which quality cannot fall. Teacher quality is much more likely to be driven by changes in the workplace—productivity enhancements, compensation improvements, more professional leadership and management—

than by requirements for how teachers are trained before or during their careers.

This is not to say that there are not promising models of teacher preparation and in-service training—including Peabody, as we shall see. But we know far too little to mandate any single approach to teacher preparation and credentialing. Instead of trying to provide quality assurance through licensure, policymakers should provide quality assurance by measuring performance directly. Policy should provide for the direct measurement of teacher effectiveness *and* the direct measurement of training effectiveness. Training programs might be university-based or not, pre-service or in-service. The effectiveness of each should be gauged by the ability of participants subsequently to raise student achievement. Once the effectiveness of programs is objectively determined and made public, prospective teachers and employers will patronize those programs that work and eschew those that do not. In time, successful training programs will replicate and replace unsuccessful ones. Policymakers need not mandate them. Policymakers should focus instead on providing districts, schools, and principals with strong incentives to select, develop, and retain well-trained and high-performing teachers.

Moving beyond licensing and other regulatory approaches to teacher quality will not be easy. The status quo does not change readily in education. Over the years it has resisted innovation in countless ways, including technology, training, accountability, compensation, and more. The strategy advanced here is surely a threat to influential interests in the educational system, from teachers' unions to schools of education. It promises to cut teaching positions and put ineffective education schools out of business. It also offers benefits. Teaching *can* become more professional and better compensated. University-based training *can* play a serious role in teacher development. In the past, the cost-benefit calculation has always come down on the side of resistance. And U.S. students have paid the price in achievement. Today, there is growing consensus that teachers are the key to achievement. The next step is recognizing that achieving with the best in the world requires teaching with the best. We have a long way to go in achievement—and so too a long way to go in teaching. A very different strategy is clearly necessary, whatever the politics.

CHAPTER 2

Fewer Teachers, Better Teachers

The instructional model employed in U.S. schools today is broken. Teachers have much more training than ever before. Sixty percent hold master's degrees, which is more than double the rate in 1971.[1] Teachers are responsible for far fewer students at a time: pupil-teacher ratios have dropped from 22.3 pupils per teacher in 1971 to 15.5 in 2011. Elementary class sizes dropped from an average of twenty-seven to twenty-two, and departmentalized teachers in elementary and secondary schools went from serving 135 students to serving only eighty-seven on average.[2] Teachers have twice as much experience—fifteen years versus eight.[3]

Yet student achievement has been disappointing at best. Long term trends on NAEP show some progress in reading and math by nine- and thirteen-year-olds, but seventeen-year-old students, wrapping up their high school careers, have exactly the same achievement today as in 1971.[4] Internationally, U.S. students are significantly behind many countries with which the United States must compete economically. In the most recent report from the Programme for International Student Assessment (PISA) on achievement among fifteen-year-olds, the United States ranked twenty-fourth in reading, thirty-first in math, and twenty-third in science among seventy developed and developing nations.[5]

There are many influences on achievement, of course. Schools arguably have a tougher job today, with higher rates of single-parent households, second-language learners, and students with special needs. But, it is impossible to ignore the sizable efforts that have been made to make the traditional model work—more teachers, more education, more experience—and not conclude it is a failing strategy.

Where the strategy goes wrong is in assuming that the quality of instruction will improve through reductions in teacher workload or increases in formal education and classroom experience. Research has demonstrated conclusively that incremental reductions in class size have little effect on achievement, that experience is of no benefit after the first few years of teaching, and that a master's degree has no effect on student achievement.[6] Clearly a different model of quality instruction is needed.

The Dilemma of Whole-Group Instruction

Teachers in the United States and, for that matter, around the world work with students primarily through a model of what is known as whole-group instruction. A teacher is assigned a class of students—which might be as few as twenty students in some U.S. primary grades or as high as forty or more students in Japanese and South Korean high schools. The teacher is solely responsible for the learning of the students in the class. This includes preparing lessons, teaching lessons, and assessing student progress. It also means creating a physical environment that supports teaching and learning, managing student behavior, maintaining student records, interacting with parents, and more. This is a challenging job, and always has been. Teachers in the United States have not become any better at it, despite the reductions in class size, the new master's degrees, and the additional experience.[7]

But this is not really surprising. The model of whole-group instruction comes with an inherent challenge that current tactics do little to address. Students who make up the typical whole group are a diverse lot. Particularly in disadvantaged communities, where students may not receive much educational reinforcement at home, students bring to school a range of learning deficits: limited vocabulary, lack of familiarity with formal oral English, poor concepts of print (such as how English is arranged on a page), and so forth. These deficits make effective instruction difficult. But the difficulty is exacerbated by the *range* of deficits that students in any classroom will likely possess. In a second grade classroom, for example, it is not unusual to find a large group of students with kindergarten level skills, another group with first grade skills, and a third group achieving at or above grade level.

The heterogeneity of students involved in whole-group instruction creates a host of problems for the teacher. Lesson planning must be "differentiated" so that instruction can target needs at multiple levels—which is time-consuming and intellectually challenging. Instruction itself must reach multiple audiences. Assignments must allow students at different levels to demonstrate their progress. These accommodations do not always get made. Teachers frequently "teach to the middle," lacking either the time or the knowledge to customize instruction for each group in the room. But this can be counterproductive. Students for whom lessons are too difficult can become frustrated, act out, and disrupt the learning of others. Students for whom lessons are too easy can become bored and disengaged, and fail to progress close to their potential.

Schools sometimes address the heterogeneity problem by grouping students by ability. This may be done for a single subject, such as primary reading. Or it may affect a whole program of study, as in college prep and general tracks in high school. But these remedies come with their own side effects; students in the lower groups seem to suffer from the absence of academically successful students as role models. The subject of student grouping and tracking is among the most studied (and politicized) topics in education research. The evidence points to no best practice for overcoming the dilemma of whole-group instruction: how can schools help students with a range of aptitude and achievement learn to their full potential, when students must be instructed in large groups?[8]

KIPP Empower Academy

KIPP LA Schools is a charter management organization that oversees five KIPP schools in the Los Angeles area. In 2009, it recruited Mike Kerr, of Brooklyn, New York, to open its new KIPP Empower Academy (KEA) in South Los Angeles, a disadvantaged neighborhood only blocks from where the 1992 Rodney King riots began.[9] Kerr had served for five years as the founding principal of the Achievement First Crown Heights Elementary School. During his tenure the school became one of the highest achieving schools in the entire state of New York, with 95 percent of students reaching proficiency on state reading and math exams in third grade and 99 percent in fourth grade.

Kerr attributed his success in Brooklyn to intensive small group instruction. He hired sufficient teachers to staff every class with two teachers. Students were taught core subjects in groups of similar ability with an average size of about ten students, smaller for less able students, larger for more able. Teachers focused their whole instructional time on one level of need, taught intensely, assessed students frequently, and regrouped them based on progress when necessary. No group was allowed to fall behind as teachers shared responsibility for students at all levels. Kerr could afford this strategy because New York provided his charter school $13,000 per student in funding. He intended to use the same strategy at KEA.

California school finance is not as generous, however. And shortly after his arrival, Kerr found his new state becoming even tighter. Before taking the post with KIPP, Kerr had laid out a plan to staff KEA with extra teachers to reduce core group size. But in 2009, reeling from the recession, California eliminated class-size reduction funding for new and expanding charter schools and reduced other school spending. The result was a cut in the school's first year budget of $200,000. Like all KIPP schools, KEA was planned to open small, beginning with just kindergarten, and grow one grade at a time. With a first year enrollment projected at only 100 students, the cut amounted to 15 percent of Kerr's anticipated budget. California funding would not support anything like the small group instructional model that Kerr had used in New York.

But Kerr was undeterred. He had to find some way to get core instructional groups down dramatically in size. His answer turned out to be technology. Kerr was hardly a true believer. He had researched education technology and found most of the providers focused on high school. As he probed deeper, he found what appeared to be promising software for primary students, but no one provider handled all subjects well. Kerr also worried about the ability of primary students as young as age five to manage multiple user names and passwords as they launched one provider's software, then another's. Kerr also feared overload for teachers, first helping children employ technology, then making sense of all of the data on student progress that the various programs would provide them.

In time, Kerr found support from a veteran of online education. Anthony Kim, the president of Education Elements, a new educational technologies consulting firm, had cut his teeth on software development for one of the largest full-time online charter schools in the United States, Pennsylvania Cyber Charter School.[10] Kim had helped that institution, based in western Pennsylvania, develop its online platform and grow to 8,000 students—in large part by creating a pleasing online experience for students and teachers.[11] KEA enlisted Kim and Education Elements to build a single sign-on system for students and a dashboard for teachers, integrating online instructional programs and common assessments into one seamless package.

None of this was easy, being invented as they went. But KEA opened its kindergarten in September 2010, with enough of the technology in place to facilitate small group instruction. Key to the model is the placement of computers. Rather than the customary model of computers in a lab to which students travel for online instruction, Kerr insisted that the computers be located in the classrooms. There, teachers would work with groups of students rotating from computer stations to face-to-face small group instruction. With computers in the classroom, teachers could also more easily maintain a consistent learning environment and disciplinary model, and not sacrifice instructional time traveling to a lab.

In its first year, the school included four classrooms of twenty-nine students—up by nearly half from the twenty students per class first envisioned. Each classroom has a lead teacher. Each pair of classrooms also shares an "intervention teacher." The intervention teachers alternate between two classrooms, providing an extra teacher for math and reading. With fifteen computers per classroom, the twenty-nine students can be divided into three small groups for reading and math, two with teachers and one with the computers. During instructional time, students rotate from teachers to computers. Reading groups are as small as six students. Writing and science instruction follow a similar model, but without an intervention teacher. Instead, an instructional aide, who is shared by each pair of classrooms, is in the room to provide additional adult support while the lead teacher instructs small student groups. As in his Brooklyn school, Kerr asks teachers to focus instruction laser-like on the needs of each small group, to teach intensely whatever the level, to assess progress often, and to regroup frequently, ensuring all students receive the instruction that they need.

The financials for this model are straightforward. Kerr reduced his originally planned core teaching staff by one teacher, dropping from five to four, thereby saving one teacher's salary and benefits. He added sixteen students to the school, raising enrollment from 100 to 116 students—with four classes of twenty-nine instead of five classes of twenty. He bought sixty computers instead of twenty. Table 1 summarizes the first year budget impact. Overall, Kerr saved $121,500 for kindergarten, a little over $1,000 per student—on total per pupil funding just north of $9,000 per student. The savings more than made up for the loss of class-size reduction funds and saved the school more than 10 percent of its anticipated costs.

Table 1: KEA Kindergarten Budgets 2010–2011 Traditional versus Hybrid Learning

	Traditional	Hybrid	Impact
Teachers per Grade Level	5	4	
Payroll Headcount	14	13	+$72,000
Classrooms/Furniture	5	4	+$20,000
Students	100	116	+$147,000
Increased Misc. Costs			−$25,000
Computers	20	60	−$40,000
Software Licenses	$2,500	$25,000	−$22,500
Tech Consultants, PD		$30,000	−$30,000
ESTIMATED SAVINGS PER GRADE LEVEL			+$121,500
ESTIMATED SAVINGS PER STUDENT			+$1,047

Serving students in South Los Angeles—Compton, Inglewood, South-Central—KEA has a high level of economic disadvantage: 95 percent of its students qualify for free- or reduced-price lunch. Students predictably entered the school well below grade level in achievement. Over 60 percent scored "below basic" on the Chicago STEP assessment of literacy, used by the school to identify instructional needs. At year's end, achievement levels were remarkably higher. On the nationally norm-referenced SAT-10, 96 and 92 percent of students scored in the top quartile in reading and math, respectively. On the Northwest Evaluation Association (NWEA) MAP assessment, the most widely used formative assessment tool in public schools today, 96 percent of students scored above the national average, with the vast majority in the top quartile.

KIPP schools have a number of positive influences on achievement—longer school days and a relentlessly positive culture among the most apparent. It is impossible to say what exactly produced student success at KEA. In each core subject students spent about fifteen to thirty minutes per day with technology and another thirty to sixty minutes in intense small group instruction. The instruction overall was clearly effective, though there is no telling how or why the particular blend of teachers and technology succeeded.

Teachers, initially fearful of the larger class sizes, in the end were very satisfied with the experience. The school out-performed most KIPP schools nationwide. KEA teacher satisfaction was 4.63 on a 5-point scale; all other KIPP schools averaged 3.93. Teachers reported that they appreciated most the chance that very small groups provided to get to know their students. Parents, also nervous about the large class sizes in the beginning, gave the school high marks in the end as well—4.71 versus 4.36 for KIPP schools nationally.

This is a small-scale experiment, in its first year. But first years are often rocky for school initiatives of any kind, especially ones as ambitious as this. The school grew into first grade in 2011–2012, and enrolls 232 students. The school is organized according to the same principles as was kindergarten. The economics are a little better, however, as grades above kindergarten do not include aides. The technology works better in year two than year one, as might be expected. The school is on track to grow to 550 students serving grades K–4.

As the school grows, Kerr said he hopes he can identify stronger online instructional programs or that better ones emerge. The public education system has been slow to adopt technology that might perform some of the same roles as classroom teachers.[12] Elementary schools largely employ instructional software in lab settings to supplement classroom instruction, with little ability to integrate the two. Most of this software is remedial, providing extra drills for reading and math skills. These programs can be valuable for students who need them. But their failure to connect with teachers and teachers' regular curricula compromises their effectiveness. What Kerr wants and needs are programs that directly complement face-to-face curriculum and instruction. Such programs exist but, given the lack of demand, they are not as plentiful as pioneers in online learning would like.

Kerr also needs the right teachers. The blended model that he and his first-year team crafted is very different from traditional whole-group instruction. Each lead teacher must supervise a large class of students. Each lead teacher must entrust part of his or her students' instruction to another teacher—the intervention teacher. Each teacher must supervise—out of the corner of one eye—students working independently on computers. (Student management turned out not to be a problem in year one, but may be as students get older.) Teachers must adjust student groups and instruction in response to assessment data, from both classroom and online assessments. This all requires some level of intelligence, not to mention skill and flexibility.

Kerr selected his own staff, as charter school leaders are able to do. All of his first-year teachers returned. After selecting his new teachers, his staff includes half alumni of Teach for America, a very smart group, and half products of traditional schools of education, a group Kerr characterizes as "equally good." Since TFA teachers and alumni constitute much less than 1 percent of all teachers nationwide, Kerr's 50 percent TFA figure is extremely high. Regardless of pedigree, Kerr's teachers average six years of experience. This may be the most important statistic. They proved themselves successful with students before joining KEA. Kerr then hired them into KEA with full knowledge of the very different model they would be required to implement. If they wanted a small class to call their own, if they wanted traditional whole-group instruction, they needed to work somewhere else.

Alliance Technology and Math Science High School

On the east side of Los Angeles, in a largely Hispanic neighborhood, sits the new Sonia M. Sotomayor campus of the Los Angeles Unified School District, honoring the nation's first Hispanic Supreme Court justice.[13] The campus is home to three pilot schools run by the district and two charter schools. Alliance Technology and Math Science High School (ATAMS), a charter school, opened in the summer of 2011 with grades nine through eleven. Grade twelve was scheduled to be added in 2012. In its inaugural year, the school enrolled 250 students. It plans to expand to 600. Eighty-eight percent of students are Hispanic and 73 percent are eligible for free or reduced-price lunches, a high level of acknowledged poverty for a high school.

But the school operates nothing like a disadvantaged school. Every student has his or her own laptop computer. The entire school curriculum is online. Students take core courses through software provided by Compass Learning. Tutoring happens online too, through Revolution Prep, Virtual Nerd, and Khan Academy. Advanced Placement courses are delivered virtually by Apex Learning. Literacy skills are reinforced by Achieve 3000. BrainHoney provides a learning management system for customized content. These cutting-edge technology programs are among the best-regarded in the industry.

The school is part of the Alliance College-Ready Public Schools charter management organization. But its design owes much to the school's principal, Michelle Tubbs, who holds a doctorate in education technology from Pepperdine University. Her dissertation focused on teachers' use of formative assessment data to drive instruction. Alliance Schools recruited Tubbs from Loyola Marymount University, where she was a clinical professor, to become the charter organization's math director and then principal of an experimental school. Tubbs is no ivory-tower academician, however. She taught for twenty years in schools in Pennsylvania, Texas, Colorado, and California, trying out new ideas and learning from experience. ATAMS is a synthesis of ideas developed over time.

The ATAMS program provides a highly structured learning experience, based on three distinct models of instruction. First is direct instruction by teachers. Students receive core instruction in the major subject areas, face-to-face, following prescriptive curricula. Second is cooperative learning. Students work in cooperative groups of four students, with each student at a different academic level and one student the designated peer tutor.

The focus is on guided practice of the skills learned in direct instruction. Each group works through set exercises with individual assessments at the end. The third element is computer-based instruction. Each student works online on a personal laptop using instructional software tailored to individual need.

None of these elements alone is original. But together they constitute a unique design. Most distinctive: all three models take place under the supervision of a single teacher—each supervising a class of forty-eight students! The high school schedule is divided into three two-hour blocks each day except Wednesday. On Wednesday, the school dismisses early for professional development, and students meet in each of their classes for one shortened period. Four days a week, the two-hour blocks rule. It is during those blocks that students follow the tripartite rotation: forty minutes of direct instruction with the classroom teacher, forty minutes of collaborative learning, and forty minutes of personalized computer-based instruction. One day the blocks might be math, then science, then an elective; the next day English, an elective, then history. Major subjects meet twice a week plus the single period on Wednesday—the same time in total as a traditional high school, but structured very differently.

For the same reasons as expressed by Kerr, Tubbs has all instruction in one classroom under the watchful eye of a core teacher. The difference here is that each teacher is supervising forty-eight students. To make the model work, Tubbs and her staff have set up each classroom, regardless of subject matter, in the same fashion. Student assignments at each station and for each class are governed by the same color-coded "digital agendas" that make it easy for students to know what they should be doing without teacher guidance. It took a lot of planning for the school-wide management system to be put in place, and a few weeks at the beginning of school for students to get the hang of it. But mid-year it appeared to be working smoothly.

Teachers like the "class size" of sixteen students for direct instruction. The small groups allow teachers to deliver lessons that are well-targeted to student needs and to work more closely with students as individuals. Teachers are also supported with technological productivity tools. Every classroom has a smart board on which teachers can view the work of every student's laptop. The monitoring helps keep students on task. Tubbs has a large screen television in her office as well, able to access the screen of any student's laptop. Student assessment is mostly electronic, and data are gathered in one grade book for easy consumption by teachers—though integration here is still in process. Students are also kept fully informed about their own progress electronically, and tend to self-monitor and try to "beat their prior score"—a quality that technology seems to bring out more in students than traditional assessment.

The school affords its rich menu of technology with a staff that includes fewer teachers than a traditional high school serving the same number of students. With ten sections of twenty-five students, a traditional high school would use twelve core teachers. ATAMS uses only eight—a 33 percent savings. Tubbs' teachers receive as much planning and professional development time as in a traditional school. The difference is the number of students that they serve. Tubbs sold the model to teacher prospects as "only sixteen students at a time." She argues that teachers basically have trouble "letting go of control," or not owning students every minute of the day. But thoughtful teachers also know that the traditional model of teacher-supervised instruction often does not work well. Many students are not achieving and may benefit from a real alternative—which ATAMS surely offers. The key for teachers, according to Tubbs, is "checks and balances," or procedures to ensure that students use their freedom properly. And ATAMS provides this through consistent routines and frequent assessments.

It is too early to tell how well students will achieve in this model. Tubbs chose two math teachers with whom she has worked for a decade to help ensure success. She hand-picked the other six teachers, all veterans with track records of helping students succeed. She also has evidence from a pilot that she operated for the Alliance network before opening ATAMS. The school bears close attention. It is pushing the envelope of student autonomy and customized learning. It is trading a large share of a school's human capital for teaching technology. It is offering the innovation to a community that otherwise does not have extensive access to technology. In a local television program highlighting the school's opening, students were effusive about the opportunity. They seem to know, if only instinctively, that something vastly different from their old high schools is needed.

San Jose Charter Academy

In a working class section of West Covina, California, on the eastern edge of Los Angeles County, sits one of the most successful public schools in the entire state.[14] By all rights it should not be. When it opened in 1998, its state test scores were predominantly "below basic." Half of all students were low-income. The majority were Latino, including many English language learners. Its average class size in grades four through six was a whopping forty-one students. Yet in 2011, San Jose Charter Academy is among the elite recipients of the California Distinguished School award, and boasts achievement midway between "proficient" and "advanced." Among schools with similar demographics statewide, it ranks in the top decile.

The success of San Jose Charter Academy can be traced to one factor—or, more precisely, one person—the school principal, Denise Patton. Dr. Patton founded the school as a district-sponsored charter school in 1998 and has led the school continuously since then. She used the freedom of charter organization to put in place both fundamentals and innovations that enable students of all backgrounds to be successful. The focus of her efforts has always been her teachers—about which chapter 4 will have more to say. In recent years technology has played an increasing role in helping her teachers succeed.

But that gets a little ahead of the story.

When San Jose Charter Academy launched as a K–5 school it served only about 400 students. In 1999, after its first round of state testing, it posted an API (Academic Performance Index) score of 638. The API is California's overall index of school academic performance. It ranges from 200 to 1,000, with 800 as the state target for all schools. The index is a weighted average of student test scores in English language arts, mathematics, and, in more recent years, science and history or social studies. (Additional subjects are added in high school.) Student scores are awarded 1,000 points for "advanced" performance, 875 points for "proficient," 700 for "basic," 500 for "below basic," and 200 for "far below basic." The school's initial score of 638 placed it in the "below basic" zone, far from the state target of 800. The scores were not just low in absolute terms; they were below the average of schools with similar student challenges. Compared to comparable schools statewide, San Jose ranked in only the fourth decile.

By 2011 all of this had changed. The school's overall API rating had risen nearly 300 points, to 924 overall. With some variation by grade level and subject, students averaged 85 percent "proficient" or "advanced" school-wide. And, the school was much bigger. Middle school grades were added soon after opening. Enrollment grew from 400 students to 1,160. It was a major task helping this many students succeed, at ever increasing rates— but the school did. The API score rose steadily every year.

Success found students of every type. When NCLB introduced its accountability measure, AYP (Adequate Yearly Progress), the school met those escalating standards, too. Every student sub-group did as well. In a school of this size, most racial, ethnic, or income subgroups will have enough students to provide statistically significant measures and "count" toward AYP. In 2011, San Jose satisfied all eleven of its school-wide and subgroup AYP standards.

The local community recognizes this success. The school has a waiting list of 1,800 students. Like a scene out of the award-winning 2010 movie, *Waiting for Superman*, the principal and staff have to console hundreds of crestfallen families when their names are not chosen in the annual enrollment lottery. As Patton puts it, everyone "wants to be part of something that is really special."

This most certainly includes the teachers. Patton notes with pride that nearly every teacher and staff member at the school has his or her own children enrolled in San Jose. Over the last four years Patton has not lost a single teacher—and that from a group that numbers over seventy-five. Patton attributes the loyalty to the climate that she and fellow school leaders have created to support teacher success. That support must be powerful indeed. Teachers at San Jose work an eight-hour day, giving students seven and a half hours of daily instruction. That is an hour and a half more instruction than district public schools. Patton is only able to pay her teachers the same wages as traditional local schools. By her estimates, her average teacher is "underpaid by $15,000 per year." Class sizes remain large. While grades K–3 have classes with only twenty students—to receive state class-size reduction funds—grades four through eight average thirty-four students.

Yet teachers could not be more committed to the school, or more successful in their teaching. Patton attributes both to the support that she has learned to provide her teachers over time. Every year she asks herself, "If I am going to ask teachers to achieve really high expectations, what do I need to do *above* those expectations to support them?" Lately, some of that support has come in the form of technology.

From its inception, San Jose was a pioneer with technology. As a part of the Edison Schools network (now EdisonLearning), San Jose provided early students with home computers—well before computers were commonplace in homes.[15] The school implemented an online formative assessment system that Edison designed to provide monthly diagnostic and predictive information to help teachers help students meet state standards. The staff was data-savvy before data came into educational vogue. But instruction was still done largely the old-fashioned way—via whole class instruction. In classrooms with sometimes forty or more students, that was beyond challenging. In 2008, San Jose became a pilot for a blended learning model developed by Edison Schools.

The idea was to use technology to provide differentiated instruction, to supplement what the teacher was accomplishing in the regular classroom. The model involved the creation of large learning spaces: computer labs, library media centers, and "flex labs" with computers and places for small group instruction and cooperative learning projects. When students were in these large learning spaces, their instruction would be tailored to their individual needs, whether delivered by computer, teacher, or other students. Edison built these novel learning spaces in three charter schools: San Jose Charter Academy, plus two in Dayton, Ohio.[16]

At San Jose, two large computer labs were built, each able to accommodate sixty-eight students at a time. Students sit at pentagonal tables or pods, with dividers providing privacy between computer stations. All computers are managed through a single

LanSchool command unit that allows teachers to monitor all students' computer screens simultaneously. (No checking Facebook undetected.) Students work on a range of individually assigned educational technology programs. Achieve 3000 and KidBiz are used to develop reading comprehension and writing skills. Lexia remediates phonics fundamentals. The Scholastic Reading Inventory provides formative assessment data and Lexile scores to help teachers assign students properly challenging readings.[17] Read 180 provides intensive reading comprehension tutorials to students in grades three through five who need the extra boost. A Scholastic Math Inventory provides formative math assessments and follow-up practice. The school's core Everyday Math program includes software for reinforcement online. The lab is supported by a single sign-on system that makes it easy for students regardless of age to access their personal assignments.

The labs are part of a daily "customized learning" block in which students rotate among computer use, small group instruction, and library media center activities. The large labs are frequented every other day by most students. All of this, according to Patton, helps teachers be more successful by taking some of the burden of differentiated instruction off of their backs and providing them lots more data about student needs to guide their work in their classrooms. The number of online programs and the access that San Jose provides its students are still unusual among America's public schools.

Also unusual are the large technological spaces. These afford teachers daily opportunity to collaborate, as two classes share the space at any one time. The idea is not for two random classes to schedule in at the same time, but for grade-level pairs to come to the lab together. Teachers can then support one another and their collective students as students work on computer assignments and projects. Teachers can also provide their partners free time to plan or take care of other responsibilities. This is crucial to the economics of the blended model, as well as its benefits as a teacher support. The labs are designed to be monitored by a single teacher. The pods, the customized assignments, the single sign-on, the central monitoring station—all are aimed at ensuring that students require little direct adult intervention or supervision and can work independently. In the end, students learn when they make new knowledge and skills their own, and this demands independence. One teacher can supervise sixty-eight students when conditions are right.

Patton reports that students generally are fully engaged and well-behaved in the double-sized labs. She emphasizes that the key is not technology but teacher preparation. If teachers are very thoughtful about the fit of online assignments to individual students, and if teachers follow up on lab work and hold students accountable, students are diligent with technology. Students certainly find the software attractive in its own right. If they know the assignments are also integral to their teacher's instruction, they tend to get the most out of the customized assignments. This observation reinforces what Mike Kerr and Michelle Tubbs stressed at their much smaller schools: technology works best when students see their teachers connected to it.

As in the previous two schools, training and ongoing support are necessary to help teachers integrate technology effectively. At San Jose, this is done now, as it has been done for over a decade, by near-daily professional development sessions run by teacher leaders and school support staff. Throughout America, public schools routinely provide teachers daily planning or free time. At San Jose, as they say, "not so much." At San Jose, time away from students is captured by the school for ongoing training, data analysis, and leadership meetings—all designed to keep the school moving forward, as a team, toward such school-wide goals as continued growth on the state API.

With planning time within the school day scarce, the large learning labs become an important safety valve. They provide time when a teacher can step away from his or her students, while a teammate supervises, to complete critical work that needs to get done during the school day. The labs provide time when teachers can share ideas about what is working or not working in common lessons. The labs provide time when teachers can allow students to do more of the work and them a little less. In the highly satisfying—but highly demanding— world of San Jose Charter Academy, that is time that helps teachers maintain the daily energy and morale to be top performers.

Blended learning is now an integral part of the success of San Jose. Teachers matter most, as always. But technology has made their jobs easier. It provides differentiation. It offers information. And it provides time for private planning or collaboration. It is extremely hard work teaching students seven and a half hours per day—especially when the compensation is the same as most teachers receive for teaching only six. In time Patton hopes to do something about compensation. For now, technology has helped make the job one that teachers clearly value. Students are the richer for it.

Resistance to Innovation

These three Los Angeles-area schools illustrate the potential of technology to blend with teacher-led instruction to create new educational models. They illustrate the possibility of changing instruction from the ubiquitous model of one teacher to one classroom, engaged in whole-group instruction, to approaches that are qualitatively different. These changes are potentially important for teachers as well as students.

Students have serious opportunities to experience the promise of technology: personalized paths through the curriculum, self-pacing, multi-media, intelligent tutoring, learning networks, and more. Teachers have the opportunity to teach differently and to play new roles. In two of the schools, teachers are able to instruct very small groups of students, all at the same academic level. Research on class size indicates that extremely small classes do make a significant difference for student achievement.[18] Research on reading instruction indicates that small homogeneous reading groups likewise are effective.[19] In all three schools teachers facilitate and complement work that students do online—helping their own instruction as well as the progress of students.

There is good reason, then, to think that these models may support student achievement. They represent qualitatively different approaches to teaching and learning than traditional whole-group instruction. These models are also not isolated examples. Many schools are trying out new mixtures of teaching and technology to create blended learning models. A 2011 survey of such innovations profiled sixty different experiments throughout the nation.[20] The models are distinguished by the new roles they create for teachers as well as the new opportunities they provide students to learn. The cases include non-charter schools within public school districts as well as charter schools like the three highlighted here.

School districts are not innovating rapidly, however. Most of the online instruction in regular public schools is outside of the academic core. The most common uses of computer-based instruction in public schools are credit recovery—allowing students to make up classes they failed in traditional classrooms by taking courses online; Advanced Placement—enabling students to take accelerated classes for which there is too little demand on the home campus to provide via a live teacher; drop-back-in courses—helping students who have dropped out of high school complete course work on their own time and without returning to (or disrupting) the regular high school program; and reading and math remediation drills. The first three uses are for high school students; the last, for elementary or, occasionally, middle school students. In all cases, the online instruction has little if any connection to the regular classroom teacher.[21]

There is a pattern to this process of adoption. It allows schools to take advantage of technology where it promises to be least disruptive to established operating procedures. Schools have always struggled with students who fail, drop out, need extra help—or need exceptional acceleration. Technology is a welcome solution for those needs. But for core instruction, buildings are already set up for whole-group instruction in like-size classrooms, the core curriculum is designed and purchased to be delivered by teachers, and the school system employs hundreds, if not thousands, of teachers, curriculum specialists, aides, and the like to provide a core program of whole-group instruction.

New technology takes people out of their comfort zones. Teachers understandably are not anxious to make wholesale changes in how they teach. But there is more to the sluggish progress of educational technology than teacher discomfort—which, after all, could be addressed with training and support. Like any industry, education is not anxious to change its ways if it means major changes in employment. Technology, after all, is a productivity tool. Its introduction makes it possible for people to do more than they did without technology. New technologies can sometimes do work that was previously done by people—which includes teaching an entire course. New technologies can also perform tasks that people could not feasibly do—such as analyzing mountains of student assessment data in real time to help teachers adjust their instruction. Together, these innovations allow industries to become more productive, providing improved service with fewer people at lower cost. The "fewer people" innovations tend to come the most slowly. No firm or industry wants to lay off people.

In competitive industries, firms ultimately have no choice. Firms that are able to offer better value by adopting new technologies, including those that save labor, take business from firms that are slower to adapt. Sometimes the early adopters are on the edge of established industries. Sometimes firms within an industry move quickly enough. Harvard business Professor Clayton Christensen has studied these "disruptive innovations" in numerous industries over the past two decades and recently took a look at public schools. His prediction is that the seepage of online learning into areas of "non-consumption"— places like credit recovery and remediation where employment is not at risk—will eventually demonstrate the value of technology, educationally and economically, and spur its acceptance for the academic core of public schools.[22]

Shortly after Christensen's book was published, Terry Moe and I offered a different forecast.[23] Public education is not a competitive industry. It is more like an economic monopoly, with each school district able to do what it likes as long as it can satisfy the political authorities—local boards and state legislatures—that oversee it. Education politics tend to be dominated by the teachers and other employees of the public education system. Teachers' unions are the richest and most powerful political organizations in every state.[24] They don't win on all issues, of course, but they have a significant say, especially when the issues concern jobs. Technology is about jobs.

In the book we detail the efforts made by teachers' unions and other representatives to block the introduction of technology into public schools. The issue is not just slow adoption of technology in schools; it is outright opposition to its introduction. Full-time online education, for example, has been fought tooth and nail by the establishment, if it is to be offered by anyone other than the school district. School systems do not want to lose "their" students and their revenue—and the jobs that those revenues support—to other schools. So, online charter schools have been fought fiercely. While thirty-eight states and the District of Columbia now permit online charter schools, the vast majority of states impose such severe restrictions on them that only a handful of states enroll the preponderance of students.[25] No state funds its online charters at levels equal to brick-and-mortar schools, even though they all fulfill the same responsibilities. Nationwide, only about 200,000 students— from a population of over 50 million in public schools—are enrolled in full-time online charters.

Full-time online education is not for everyone. Most families do not have the luxury of having a parent stay at home to supervise full-time online instruction. Families also tend to value the socialization experience of a brick-and-mortar school. But there are many students for whom traditional schools do not work—students who eventually drop out because they are frustrated or embarrassed by their deficits in a traditional classroom; students who have been bullied and fear regular school attendance; highly achieving students whose needs simply are not being met in regular classes; athletes and performing artists who desire more time and flexibility to pursue their passions while also being educated; and special needs students who benefit from technology. There are also 2 million students already being home-schooled.[26] So, it is likely the demand for full-time online learning far exceeds the 200,000 students now enrolled. The supply is being politically suppressed.

The big market for online education, however, is not full-time. It is part-time—and not from home, but from school. Every public school student stands to benefit from the expanded use of technology in education. Technology can remediate, accelerate, and provide customized practice; it can expose students to worlds of information and provide access to star teachers anywhere on the planet; it can bring alive concepts through multimedia displays and interactive programs that classrooms cannot duplicate; and it enables every student to move at his or her own pace and on his or her own path through a curriculum. Students can experience technology through whole courses taken online, or through programs that are integrated with instruction by live teachers at school. Public schools can become hybrid institutions where learning occurs through interaction with teachers and technology, blended in ways that are just beginning to be discovered.

Progress to date has been slow. Only three states require students to take a course online to receive a high school diploma—preparation for a high tech future. But when one of those states, Idaho, upped the requirement to two courses, the political backlash from the state teachers' union was so intense it made front page news in the *New York Times*.[27] The majority of states (forty-five, to be exact) have created state-sponsored online schools from which students anywhere in a state can take courses. In 2011, students participated in 450,000 semester courses. Half of these courses, however, were taken from one state online school, Florida Virtual School. This is because Florida law gives all high school students the right to take any course online—without their schools' permission. In other states, school permission is required and enrollment is controlled.[28] As a rule, online education is still very much governed by the decisions of districts and schools about how much access they wish to offer. If the district wants to provide students access to Apex Learning for Advanced Placement or Achieve 3000 for literacy support, or a host of other resources, that is its prerogative. Progress therefore follows the path of least political resistance. Most students have limited access.

Raising Teacher Quality

Increasing student access will be a drawn-out political battle. In time, technological innovation will win. More technology will mean fewer educators, and fewer educators will mean less political influence on their part. But this process could be accelerated if policymakers and educators would recognize the benefits that technology can bring to educators themselves. Technology is not about replacing teachers with laptops; it is about making them and other education professionals more successful . . . or at least it should be.

The traditional model of instruction is not making anyone more successful. Teachers are not becoming more effective—students are not learning more—through incremental reductions in class size or incremental increases in teacher pay tied to advanced degrees or years of experience. If policymakers want to raise teacher quality, they must look at new ways to help teachers be more successful. Technology has the potential to do this. We've looked in detail at some of the ways. By taking some of the responsibility for instruction off of teachers, technology makes it possible for teachers to work with much smaller groups of students—which research suggests may boost achievement. Small groups can also be homogeneous—which reading research suggests may be effective. And the evidence is growing that online instruction itself can be more effective than traditional classrooms.[29] New blends of teachers and technology *can* raise achievement. New blends can help teachers be more successful.

New blends can do something else for teacher quality as well. New blends can help bring to the teaching profession candidates with greater potential for success. Teacher potential is difficult to predict from the resumes of new teachers.[30] Indeed, the only attributes of new teachers that research has found consistently to matter are verbal aptitude and, for prospective secondary teachers in some subjects, a college major in the field to be taught.[31] This creates a huge challenge for teacher quality, placing much of the burden on what happens to teachers after they are hired—training, retaining, and shedding teachers to maximize the effectiveness of the teaching pool. Subsequent chapters will address this challenge. But what about the quality of new recruits?

The United States has been working for a generation to raise academic standards for students. The nation wants more students achieving at the highest levels internationally and more students excelling in math and science—from which highly skilled jobs and economic growth are most likely to grow. The states have come together in recent years in the Common Core project to try to raise standards above those that many states established to comply with No Child Left Behind and, arguably, avoid sanctions for low achievement.[32] States like Massachusetts, which set their standards and proficiency levels close to the expectations of NAEP, are viewed as models that all states should try to emulate. U.S. students are a long way from meeting NAEP standards. Generalizing across grade levels, only about a third of U.S. students are proficient or better in math and reading. Whether NAEP standards are precisely the right target for U.S. schools is debatable, of course. But there is no question that the United States is aiming to raise standards for students to much greater heights.

But what about the teachers who need to help students reach these standards? We know that teachers fall well below NAEP standards. As noted earlier, studies have equated the scores of students on NAEP and on the SAT.[33] The scores that U.S. teachers post on the SAT on average—low 500s in math and critical reading for elementary teachers, about 575 for secondary math teachers—translate into "basic" scores on NAEP. The proficient level on NAEP translates into at least a 600 on the math SAT scale.[34] It is surely a challenge for teachers who lack the skills themselves to teach students to levels above their own. Research supports this proposition, even if aptitude or achievement is but one predictor of teacher success. High-achieving nations are also known to channel many of their strongest high school students into teaching.[35]

Generations ago, the United States channeled higher achieving students into teaching as well. Prior to the 1970s, teaching was the career of choice for many bright young women. Most other professions were either closed to or less open to women, and so women became teachers (or nurses or secretaries) almost by default. Over the last forty years, anti-discrimination laws and changes in attitudes have opened doors to women in traditionally male-dominated professions. Professions other than teaching have also raised compensation relative to teaching. Whereas teachers once earned over 80 percent of the wages of other college graduates, today teachers earn about 65 percent.[36] Teachers work fewer hours than most other professionals and have generous retirement benefits. But, on balance, teaching has become a relatively less attractive position economically. Women working outside of teaching have seen their wages grow faster than men's in the years since. For economic and professional reasons, the caliber of women going into teaching has fallen over the last two generations.[37] Women with the very best high school grades and test scores have been the ones who have vacated teaching at the highest rates.[38] U.S. schools attract weaker women into teaching now than a generation ago.

The United States should once again aim to attract higher-aptitude candidates into teaching. This is true whether the candidates are fresh college graduates or older career changers. The standards this nation wants students to meet call for higher-aptitude teachers. Evidence from the traditional model of teaching indicates that teacher aptitude promotes student achievement. The models of instruction that are envisioned for the future will demand even more from teachers. The role of teachers in blended models will no longer be just the whole-group instructor. Teachers will provide direct instruction, integrate technology-based instruction into face-to-face lessons, analyze assessment data from multiple sources, and provide some manner of instruction or tutoring online as well. As the next chapter will argue, teaching should be an intellectually demanding enterprise regardless of technology. Technology increases those demands, and should raise the bar for expectations of teacher quality.

The Teacher-Technology Dividend

Technology promises to make teachers more successful and more productive. Technology should make it possible for fewer teachers to help a given number of students achieve at higher levels. If nothing else in the economics of public education were to change, investments in technology could be paid for through reductions in the number of teachers. More than that, the required investment in technology can be much less than the savings in teacher compensation. Changing the mix of teachers and technology can, in fact, pay a substantial dividend. Policymakers and taxpayers would be the ones to decide how the dividend would be spent. Arguably, some of the dividend should go to improving the compensation of teachers, to attract and retain higher-caliber talent in the profession.

By international standards, the United States spends as much as—if not more than—any country in the world on education. On average, nations that belong to the Organization for Economic Co-operation and Development (OECD) spend 3.3 percent of gross domestic product (GDP) on public K–12 education.[39] The United States spends 3.7 percent, which is more than most every OECD nation, including Finland, Japan, South Korea, Germany, and Canada—nations that lead the United States in student achievement. On a per-pupil basis, the United States is also a top spender, ranking second or third in elementary and secondary spending, ahead of OECD averages by about 25 percent—and ahead of higher achieving nations.[40] It is difficult to argue that the United States needs to spend more in order to invest in technology or to improve public schools more generally. Enough is spent already. The United States is simply not getting the same bang for its buck as other nations spending less or the same.

Now, it is certainly true that the United States is a much bigger, more diverse nation than many of its economic competitors. The schooling challenge may be greater. Still, there is evidence that the United States does not spend as wisely as others. This is glaringly true of teacher compensation. Teacher salaries in the United States, when compared to GDP, are lower than twenty-four other OECD nations when their salaries are compared with their respective GDPs, for teachers with fifteen years of experience. For starting salaries, the United States is behind a majority of OECD nations.[41] In other countries teaching is a relatively more attractive job, at the beginning of a career and after lots of experience, than it is in the United States. The high level of school spending in the United States is not allocated as generously to teachers as it is in other nations—and again, nations that achieve more than the United States. For some countries, the difference lies in higher pupil-teacher ratios that allow higher wages for individual teachers.[42] Elsewhere, the difference is less money spent on school system support staff and administration, where the United States spends a great amount.[43] Whatever the reasons, many countries have chosen to give larger shares of their public education spending to individual teachers.

Compensation is hardly the only factor that attracts and retains teachers, or any professionals, in their jobs. But it is surely one factor. By restructuring the traditional model of schooling—and doing nothing else about how U.S. public schools spend their funds—the United States could reduce substantially the number of teachers required in public education. With fewer high-quality teachers to recruit, develop, and retain, the teacher quality problem becomes easier to solve. The reduction in teachers would save money that could be used in whole or in part to make compensation more attractive to teachers. The potential here is huge.

Consider the following simple model. Imagine that students receive their education partly through face-to-face instruction from teachers and partly through technology. The organizational model for this could be the within-classroom set-ups seen in the KIPP Empower Academy and the Alliance Technology and Math Science High School, or the large laboratory environment seen in San Jose Charter Academy. Assume that students in elementary school receive one hour of online instruction per day, middle school students two hours per day, and high school students three hours per day. This is a conservative estimate of what is already known to be possible today.

If students are working in large computer labs, assume they are being supervised by regular teachers, but in double-size groups in elementary and middle school and triple-size groups in high school. If students are working in the large computer labs, supervising teachers are doing no additional instruction during that time. If we further assume that the school day includes six hours of instruction for students and five hours of instruction (and one free hour) for teachers, the introduction of online learning yields the following savings in teacher

FTEs (full-time equivalents): 7 percent fewer teachers in elementary school, 14 percent fewer in middle school, and 29 percent fewer in high school.[44]

These same savings could be achieved by the online model that keeps students in their regular classrooms with their regular teachers. The savings would come by adding students to the regular classrooms, who would divide time between online learning and teacher-led instruction. More students in each classroom would reduce the number of classrooms and classroom teachers. To achieve these savings, elementary classrooms would need to add 8 percent more students per classroom, middle schools 16 percent more students, and high schools 34 percent more students. Given that the current U.S. class size average across all grades is twenty-two students, these additions would yield classes of twenty-four in elementary school, twenty-six in middle school, and thirty in high school. These are not large by the standards of blended learning models—or of some high-achieving nations with traditional classroom instruction.[45]

The overall savings in teacher FTEs across all grade levels works out to 15.4 percent fewer teachers overall. This, remember, is just from part-time online learning. Savings can also be achieved from students in full-time online learning. Currently only 200,000 students participate in full-time online learning throughout the United States, and most of that is in online charter schools. If policymakers authorized online charter schools in all states, and funded them adequately, it is easy to imagine enrollments increasing to 1 million students. Recall that 2 million students are already home-schooled, representing a natural constituency for full-time online schools. One million students amount to about 2 percent of all public school enrollments. If 2 percent of all students left traditional public schools, the need for traditional teachers could also be reduced

by 2 percent. Added to the savings from part-time online learning, the savings in teacher FTEs from education technology
could be 17.4 percent in traditional public school teachers.
These and subsequent calculations are summarized in Table 2.

Table 2: Estimated Impacts of a National Model of Blended Learning

Elements of Blended Learning Model	Impact	% of Current Expenditures	National Savings
Elementary: 1 hr/day online	7% fewer teachers		
Middle: 2 hrs/day online	14% fewer teachers		
HS: 3 hrs/day online	29% fewer teachers		
K–12: 1.85 hrs/day online	15.4% fewer teachers		
1 Million Full-Time Online	2% fewer teachers		
Part- and Full-Time Online	17.4% fewer teachers	10.6%	560K teachers
Elementary Site Licenses	$100/student		
Middle Site Licenses	$200/student		
HS Site Licenses	$300/student		
HS Additional Computers	$55/student		
All New Technology K–12	$202/student	(1.8%)	
Full-Time Lost Revenue	85% per pupil revenue	(1.7%)	
Net Savings		7.1%	$39B
Per Teacher After RIF*			$14,662
Per Top Teacher After RIF*			$28,324

*Reduction in Force of teachers from current 3.2 million to 2.62 million

By last hard count, in 2008, the United States employed
3,219,458 public school teachers.[46] A reduction of 17.4 percent
in that total is 560,185. This reduction is potentially important for many reasons. First is sheer numbers. It will be very
hard to find over 3.2 million high-quality teachers. The job
will be easier if the goal is over half a million fewer. The public schools lose about 8–10 percent of the teaching pool each
year, largely through attrition.[47] The National Center for
Education Statistics estimates that public schools will need
to hire up to 350,000 new teachers per year through 2020.[48]
That represents over 20 percent of the number of new bachelor's degrees granted currently per year in the United States.[49]

One in five new graduates will need to become teachers if that is the primary supply. The annual need for new teachers also exceeds the total number of bachelor's degrees and master's degrees granted each year in the field of education.[50]

Now, the pool of potential new teachers is not limited to these sources; many teachers who left teaching at one time are available to return. Nonetheless, the public schools are now structured to require a high percentage of educated Americans to make teaching a career. A major reduction in the number of teachers required in public education would reduce the pressure on the labor market and allow public schools to be more selective about hiring and retention.

The reduction in teachers could also pay a handsome dividend. To calculate it, the cost of technology must first be factored in. Full-time online education is funded at wide-ranging rates today. Experts estimate that online education, all-in, might cost 85 percent of brick-and-mortar education.[51] This could change over time as online education gains experience. But using the 85 percent figure, a movement of 2 percent of public school students out of traditional public schools would cost traditional schools 1.7 percent in funding.

Part-time online education requires site licenses for educational programs—which are dropping rapidly in price. Current estimates are $100 per student for elementary students, $200 for middle school students, and $300 for high school students. Computer penetration in public schools is already one computer for every three students, enough to handle the proposed elementary and middle school programs.[52] Additional computers would be needed to reduce ratios to 1:2 in high school. Those additional machines would amount to no more than $55 per student per year amortized.[53] The incremental cost of the high school program then becomes $355 per student. With six grade levels in elementary schools, three in middle schools, and four in high schools, the weighted average incremental cost of the part-time program would be $202 per student. As a proportion of current per-pupil spending, averaging about $11,000 per year nationally, the cost of a part-time technology program would be 1.8 percent. Add that to the full-time online program, and technology would consume about 3.5 percent of public school revenue.

Turning back to teachers, the last hard estimate of the total cost of teacher compensation was made in 2008, when the sum was $308 billion.[54] That represented 61 percent of "current expenditures" on public education and 52 percent of "total expenditures," which include capital outlays.[55] Those percentages have been stable for the last decade. Today, rough estimates of current expenditures are $550 billion. If we assume that the potential reduction in teacher FTEs of 17.4 percent comes at the average teacher salary—which it would in time—the financial savings in current expenditures from the reduced head count would be 61 percent of 17.4 percent—or 10.6 percent. This savings would then need to pay 3.5 percent for new technology. The dividend from trading teachers for technology would be 7.1 percent.

That is not a small sum. It's $39 billion per year. That could be used any number of ways. One could be to improve teacher compensation. The reduced pool of teachers would now number only 2.66 million. If every penny of savings were divided among all 2.66 million teachers, compensation could be increased $14,662 per teacher per year. That is a more than 25 percent increase over current average salaries of $54,800.[56] It would be bad policy to raise every teacher's salary, regardless of performance. The math simply illustrates how much better compensated teachers could be if technology were allowed to introduce savings.

Imagine, more creatively, that the $39 billion in savings were devoted to a performance compensation system, reserved for the top performing half of all teachers.[57] Then, the best teachers would be rewarded with bonuses of more than $29,000 apiece—or increases of more than 50 percent. Total compensation approaching $85,000 per year would put teacher earnings in the zone that market research indicates would be attractive to "top third" college students.[58] Washington, D.C., recently began awarding bonuses to its most effective teachers—as much as $15,000 per year. The school system made headlines doing so.[59] However it is allocated, the money is there to change compensation more radically and more widely, if teachers perform.

Fewer Teachers, Better Teachers

The current model of instruction has exhausted its ability to bring improvement for students. Technology should be employed to develop new models in which students learn more on their own and teachers perform different roles with students, sometimes more intensively and in smaller groups than is the norm today. Effective teaching under any model is an intellectually demanding pursuit, and the United States should aim to increase the academic aptitude of those recruited into the profession, especially given the likely evolution of teaching into a more technologically sophisticated field. The nation will do itself a favor if it uses technology to reduce sharply the number of teachers needed in public education. It will be far easier to find and keep great teachers if the numbers are not so large. It will also be possible to compensate them commensurate with their performance and with the stature of the profession teaching needs to become.

CHAPTER 3

Developing Great Teachers

Teacher quality is one of the great mysteries of education research. Research has established that individual teachers have substantially different effects on student achievement, effects that can accumulate and even affect lifetime earnings. But important as this effect is, research has not been able to identify what exactly it is about teachers that brings them success or failure.[1] In a recent white paper, the National Academy of Education reviewed the evidence on teacher quality and called for more experimentation—and research.[2] This puts policymakers in quite a conundrum. They know that quality teachers may be the most important cause of student learning—within the factors that fall under the control of schools. But they have no idea how to develop them.

Yet, around the world, countries succeeding with students move with confidence to recruit and train teachers.[3] In the United States, organizations outside of the traditional world of teacher education, like Teach for America and The New Teacher Project, have worked for many years now to create alternative models of teacher preparation—for which there is some evidence of success.[4] Certain university-based teacher education programs, like Vanderbilt's Peabody College, have taken steps that seem to be working. Large-scale research also offers clues, if not definitive evidence, of what strategies might hold most promise for developing high-quality teachers.

What, then, are policymakers to think? Is great teaching a mystery largely unsolved? Or are there sound steps policymakers can take to help develop the best teachers in the world?

Great Teaching Matters

Over the last decade, perhaps the most important development in education policy is the growing consensus around the importance of teacher quality. Among Democrats as well as Republicans there is now acknowledgment that the performance of *individual* teachers is critical to the success of their students. Republicans had long complained that school reform was stymied by collective bargaining agreements and civil service rules that made it impossible for principals to dismiss "bad" teachers. Democrats, speaking on behalf of their teacher union supporters, countered that teachers could not be blamed for the failures of their students and their families, principals couldn't reliably identify "bad" teachers, and that, in any case, everyone deserves due process when a job is at stake. Both parties agreed to reforms that held *schools* strictly accountable for student achievement, but teachers were omitted from the equation.

Today, thinking is different. Since taking office, President Obama and his administration have made teacher quality one of the hallmarks of education reform strategy. From the distribution of "stimulus" funds under the American Recovery and Reinvestment Act to the award of Race to the Top grants, to the approval of waivers from NCLB regulations, to its plans for the replacement of NCLB, the administration has asked states to take concrete steps to hold individual teachers accountable for student achievement.[5] The administration has insisted that state databases of student test scores identify the individual teachers responsible for each student. In 2007, only seventeen states permitted teachers to be identified in state databases. Today, virtually all states do.[6] The administration is also demanding that test scores be used as part of each teacher's annual job evaluation.

These are controversial requirements, to be sure. Democrats continue to feel pressure from unions to limit the impact of test scores on evaluations.[7] Some Republicans complain that the federal government is overreaching with these mandates, preferring states or school districts to decide how best to address teacher quality. But the progress cannot be overstated. On both sides of the partisan aisle there is strong agreement that individual teachers are critical to student achievement and that policy should help put more quality teachers in America's schools.

Research has played a major role in building this consensus. The process began with evidence as early as the 1970s, but gained steam in the 1990s.[8] At that time, Tennessee was one of the first states to test students every year in reading and math *and* track which teachers taught which students. (It was not until 2002 that NCLB required all states to test grades three through eight annually.) A team of researchers at the University of Tennessee, led by Professor William Sanders, used the data to try to separate out the effects of teachers, schools, families, and other factors on student achievement. A longstanding—and legitimate—concern among teachers was that a teacher's performance could easily be confused with factors that were not within a teacher's control. A class of students with particularly challenging home lives might make a good teacher look bad. Or an ineffective principal, one who does a poor job of maintaining school-wide discipline, might make an otherwise capable teacher appear unsuccessful. The Tennessee data covered enough factors and spanned enough school years for Sanders and his team to distinguish confidently one influence from another.

The results were nothing short of astonishing. Sanders found that individual teachers varied quite widely in their impacts on student achievement. The feeling that every parent has—that some teachers are really "good" and others really "bad"—was confirmed in the Tennessee data. Sanders called the unique effect of teachers the "value added" and calculated for each teacher a value-added score. He then ranked the teachers from lowest to highest. The 20 percent of teachers with the highest value-added scores comprised the top quintile; those with the lowest 20 percent of scores, the bottom quintile. The data showed that students working with top quintile teachers learned two to four times the amount of students working with bottom quintile teachers. The data also showed that the effects multiplied with each year a student spent with a top quintile or bottom quintile teacher. So powerful was the effect of the individual teacher that a low-performing student working with a top quintile teacher for three consecutive years could become a high-performing student. The reverse was also true; in three years a bottom-quintile teacher could seriously depress the achievement of a high-performing student.[9]

Sanders' findings attracted attention in the popular press, but didn't move school reformers. Researchers met the findings with some skepticism, and additional studies ensued. Researchers agreed that individual teachers had a significant effect on achievement, but disagreed on its magnitude.[10] Sanders' estimates appeared to be on the high end of what was real. With accountability and information systems developing in the last decade, fresh data made it possible to examine teacher quality in new settings with large numbers of students and teachers. Research on Los Angeles and New York City was particularly compelling. That work once again indicated sizable teacher effects as one-third of a standard deviation.[11] In education reform, effect sizes of this magnitude are considered large. Most recently, economists have demonstrated that the quality of an individual teacher has effects that can be felt even twenty years down the road, with top teachers eventually helping students and their classmates to substantially higher lifetime earnings.[12]

Research also offers cautions. Effect sizes are not consistent across subjects and grade levels. Effect sizes vary from one study to the next. Putting research findings into practice is also tricky, as estimates for individual teachers are not nearly as reliable as estimates for teachers as a group.[13]

Nonetheless, a consensus has emerged among policymakers that individual teachers make a very meaningful difference for student achievement: students with the same family backgrounds achieve at substantially different levels if taught by teachers of substantially different quality. Students with identical backgrounds who are lucky or unlucky enough to be taught by top quartile or bottom quartile teachers for three years running may differ by a year or more of achievement as a result.[14] This is especially relevant to economically disadvantaged students who are most likely to be taught in schools staffed by lower quality teachers. If those students could somehow be taught by top-quartile teachers for several years, the evidence suggests they could raise their achievement to grade-level standards. High-quality teachers alone might close the achievement gap.[15]

The promise of teacher quality is indeed real. The evidence that individual teachers significantly affect student achievement is overwhelmingly positive. Reformers are right to make teacher quality a priority. But what reformers should do with the evidence is another matter. Reformers should certainly try to ensure that the added value or effectiveness of teachers is rigorously gauged using student test scores. Reformers should also try to ensure that top-quartile teachers remain in teaching and that bottom-quartile teachers do not. Schools can surely be improved by better retaining top talent and shedding or "deselecting" those who are not helping students to learn.[16]

But that process would be far more efficient if schools were better at selecting high-potential teachers and helping teachers once hired to become top performers. Otherwise, our ability to measure teacher effectiveness leaves us with little more than a crude process of trial and error to improve school staffs. No successful industry hires randomly and leaves recruits to sink or swim. Yet, the evidence is that public education has actually not done much better than that. In that light, measuring effectiveness on the job, retaining, and de-selecting become major steps forward. Public education could do much better.

Teacher Education Programs That Work—and Do Not

The vast majority of teachers in U.S. public schools are trained in college- or university-based teacher education programs. Each year those schools churn out a little over 100,000 bachelor's degrees and 175,000 master's degrees in education.[17] Recipients are also recommended for licensure in the state in which the university is located. Most of the master's degrees are issued to candidates already working as teachers, who are aiming to upgrade their skills—and their compensation.[18] Research has looked carefully at this pervasive mode of training and found it wanting in the most fundamental respects. The preponderance of evidence indicates that teachers certified in this manner are no more effective than teachers uncertified or certified by other means.[19] Teachers with master's degrees are no more effective, all things being equal, than those without.[20] If a school wants to hire top-quartile teachers, certification and advanced degrees provide little or no information about prospective quality. If those are the qualifications that win the job, the probability of success is essentially random.[21]

But teacher education programs are not all the same. And the evidence is that they are not equally effective. Among U.S. colleges and universities, approximately 1,400 offer undergraduate or graduate teacher education and certification programs—three times the number of programs, correcting for population differences, as in high-performing nations like Finland and Canada.[22] The venerable Carnegie classification divides higher education institutions into "baccalaureate colleges," which focus on educating undergraduates; "master's universities," which offer master's degrees and provide some research; and "doctoral universities," which confer degrees all the way to the doctoral level and support major research. The baccalaureate colleges produce 13 percent of all undergraduate teaching degrees, master's universities produce 54 percent, and doctoral universities 33 percent. At the graduate level of teacher education, the shares are respectively 4 percent, 62 percent, and 34 percent.[23]

The bulk of training, then, is in master's and doctoral universities. The baccalaureate colleges include many selective institutions, and on average enroll prospective teachers with SAT scores above the national average for college graduates. Their aptitude bodes well for their success as teachers. The effectiveness of their training is unclear. However, the action in teacher education is not mainly in these small colleges; it's in the nation's universities. Among these nearly 800 institutions there are stark differences in likely effectiveness.

Undergraduate teaching candidates at master's universities average more than 100 points lower in combined verbal and math SAT scores than candidates at doctoral universities—1031 versus 1135. Only a third of the candidates at master's universities were at least A– students in high school; half of the candidates in doctoral universities were.[24] Faculty in master's and doctoral universities have comparable years of experience teaching in K–12 schools. But their academic caliber is vastly different. In doctoral universities, faculty are more than twice as likely to have earned their doctorates at graduate programs ranked in the top twenty nationally, and several times more likely to be active with research.[25]

Now, education schools have been frequently criticized for knowing more about research and theory than about schools and practice. But if the research being conducted is relevant to student achievement, it probably benefits teaching candidates to have faculty who are active in research. There is likewise no guarantee that faculty who are trained in top-ranked graduate programs will be better trained in what makes teachers most effective. But it is likely that faculty from stronger programs will be higher aptitude individuals, with more potential to prepare teachers to be demanding academic instructors.

These notions have been put to the test, collectively. In his comprehensive study of U.S. schools of education, Arthur Levine at Columbia contracted with the Northwest Evaluation Association (NWEA) to try to measure the effects of teacher training on student achievement. NWEA produces the most widely used formative assessment system in U.S. schools, employed by school districts in almost every state. NWEA assessments are used in reading and math from kindergarten through twelfth grade and allow schools and teachers to gauge student progress along one continuous scale. The NWEA assessments are also correlated with state tests, giving teachers perspective on student progress against state standards.

NWEA surveyed teachers in the schools using NWEA assessments on their experience as teachers and in teacher education. NWEA used the data from these surveys to try to predict growth in student reading and math scores. Growth is notoriously difficult to predict. Nonetheless, one teacher attribute proved a significant predictor: teacher experience. And, controlling for teacher experience, one attribute of teacher education also emerged as significant: the type of institution. Teachers trained at doctoral universities produced more growth in math scores and reading scores than teachers trained in master's universities. The effect sizes were not huge—0.11 in math and 0.09 in reading. But by standards of education research the differences deserve attention.[26]

Should it really come as a surprise that teachers educated in universities that are otherwise known as America's best would outperform teachers prepared in institutions that in so many ways do not measure up? Consider basic indicators. Among the top 100 doctoral universities, only one school has a freshman class with its 25th percentile below 1000 on the SAT or 21 on the ACT. Among the top 100 master's universities, a fourth have freshman classes with their 25th percentile below 1000 or 21. It is not just that education students are weaker in master's universities; students are weaker in general.[27]

Among the 100 top-ranked doctoral universities, all but ten have undergraduate graduation rates of 70 percent or above. Among the 100 top-ranked master's universities, fifty-eight have graduation rates *below* 70 percent.[28] In doctoral universities, students attend amidst a culture that supports persistence. In master's universities, graduation is not the overwhelming norm. These comparisons look at only the best 100, moreover. While there are still another 130 doctoral universities to bring down that sector's averages, there are 460 master's universities posting lower scores.

These sectors differ sharply in the students they serve and in the outcomes that they produce for them. To be fair, the performance of master's universities may have as much to do with the lower caliber of students they serve as with the programs they deliver. But it would be a surprise indeed if teachers prepared in environments where students are not strong academically and critical norms like finishing college are not in place would measure up to teachers prepared in more positive scholastic environments. Better universities are almost bound to do a better job. The United States would do well to look to them for teacher preparation. Counting on its least able universities to perform the majority of the work is simply a poor plan.

Learning from the Best

Tennessee, the birthplace of statewide value-added measurement of teacher effectiveness, is among the nation's leaders in the practice today. In 2010 the Obama administration awarded the state one of only two round-one Race to the Top grants to support work focused on the development of high-quality teachers. (Delaware was the other winner.) Tennessee has now launched a rigorous, data-based evaluation system for all teachers, veterans as well as beginners. Tennessee has also installed a value-added evaluation system for the schools that train its teachers. The most recent report is an eye-opener.

Looking at the graduates of forty-one teacher preparation programs, from 2004–2008, the analysis finds only two programs that are able to produce top teachers for the state: Peabody College at Vanderbilt University and Teach for America. Each of these programs was able to produce significantly high percentages (greater than 20 percent) of teachers performing in the top 20 percent of all teachers in the state, as gauged by value-added measures. Each program was also able to produce teachers who performed significantly better than the average of all veteran teachers in the state. The analysis studied program graduates in their first three years of teaching, about 3,400 graduates statewide annually. It examined test scores in grades three through eight for math, reading and language arts, social studies, and science. It is no small accomplishment that Peabody and TFA produced beginners who could outperform veterans and, more often than expected, match the best quintile of teachers in the state.[29]

These findings are consistent with the national picture, but based on far more relevant and rigorous analyses. They reinforce the hypothesis that talented students are crucial to successful teaching: Peabody undergraduates hold SAT scores that averaged 1438 in 2011; TFA teachers nationally averaged 1344 in 2010.[30] The study also supports converse hypotheses. Fourteen teacher preparation programs produced significantly *poorer* teachers than state averages. Their beginning teachers showed up in the bottom quintile of teachers statewide at statistically high rates; their new graduates performed significantly worse than veteran teachers; or both. The low-performing programs included many of the largest teacher preparation programs in the state: East Tennessee State University (292 new graduates), Middle Tennessee State University (338), Tennessee Technical University (374), and the University of Memphis (420). These are among the master's universities that do not fare well as a group in national perspective.[31]

Now, most teacher preparation programs in Tennessee produced teachers who performed, during their first three years on the job, at levels similar to those of teachers on the job more than three years. Given that teachers improve with early experience, being "average" is perhaps not a bad accomplishment.[32] But, Tennessee is not a high achieving state. Its NAEP reading and math scores are significantly below the national average at grades four and eight.[33] The state needs to do more than replicate past achievement, as does the nation as a whole. The state needs teachers who are top-quintile types, capable of helping students achieve at substantially higher levels. Only two programs produced teachers like that in Tennessee—Peabody College and TFA.

Teach for America has been the subject of substantial research over its more than twenty years of operation. Its effectiveness has been confirmed, though the evidence is not completely consistent.[34] The program begins with very smart, fresh college graduates and then prepares them for the opening day of school through an intense five-week boot camp. Critics of the program object that five weeks of preparation is hardly adequate for a job as challenging as teaching.[35] But the evidence is that TFA teachers somehow manage to perform as well as teachers prepared the old-fashioned way in schools of education. There is also more to TFA training than meets the eye. TFA teachers must participate in alternative certification programs while they teach and receive standard certification. They are also part of ongoing locally run TFA training programs that aim to help teachers learn from their classroom experience and not merely sink or swim.

There are lessons to be learned from TFA, if the nation is to upgrade its teaching pool. There are also limitations. TFA teachers commit to teaching for only two years. Although about half continue teaching beyond their two-year commitment, they represent a unique corps.[36] They come to their work initially with the zeal of a missionary, dedicated to help urban students for a finite period of time. They teach with an intensity born of that short-term mission. They learn what they need to learn to survive—and hopefully succeed—as fast as they possibly can. These are all great virtues. TFA teachers have come to provide an important source of fresh talent to numerous urban school systems where they focus.

But this may not be a viable large-scale source of talent. TFA currently supplies about 1 percent of the nation's new teachers each year. It and programs like it can surely expand. But its missionary recruits are a special lot. They represent young people leaving college without immediate worry about a long-term career. Today's economy does not afford this luxury to many. There is also only so much that can be learned from the experience of TFA teachers. They bring a short-term motivation to the job that for all of its virtues is unrepresentative of teachers who are committed to succeeding over the long haul. They also raise an important question: what if students this bright and dedicated were trained in a more substantial way?

Peabody College at Vanderbilt University

Founded in 1785 as Davidson Academy, and renamed twice before industrialist George Peabody gave the school a piece of his fortune and his name in 1875, Peabody College of Education and Human Development, as it is known today, is one of the nation's oldest and continuously innovative schools of education. In the early 1800s the school was led by Princeton theologian Philip Lindsley, who aimed to educate teachers in the classical tradition. During Reconstruction, George Peabody converted the college into a normal school whose mission was to train teachers who could accelerate the recovery of the South and the restoration of the Union through education. In the early to mid-1900s, after becoming a four-year institution once again and attracting a second major infusion of philanthropy—this time from John D. Rockefeller—Peabody became one of the nation's leading centers of progressive, or what it termed "practical," education. And, in the 1960s, Peabody's pre-school and special education programs became inspirations for programs nationally, including Head Start and the Special Olympics.

It was after its merger with Vanderbilt University in 1979, whose campus it adjoined, that Peabody grew into the unique institution that it is today. Since then Vanderbilt University has climbed the ranks of elite universities, transforming itself from a major regional university to an elite national university now ranked seventeenth by *U.S. News & World Report.* The middle 50 percent of its incoming freshmen range from 1330 to 1530 in SAT math and verbal scores. The university is highly selective, admitting only 18 percent of applicants.[37] Among private universities, Vanderbilt ranks in the top ten in research funding. It competes for top faculty nationally in many fields.[38]

Peabody has benefited from this association, in the same ways, and in ways that distinguish its teacher preparation programs. Peabody now ranks number one among schools of education, according to *U.S. News & World Report.*[39] Its undergraduates score at or above the high university average on the SAT. This is extremely rare, as education majors are generally at the bottom of a university's talent distribution. Its graduate students, including many in master's degree teacher preparation programs, have high GRE (Graduate Record Examinations) scores—about 1250. Peabody has more research dollars than any other school of education in the United States. Peabody's faculty members bring in more research dollars per capita than the faculty in any other school of the university, including its high-ranking medical school.[40]

Peabody College has thereby evolved into this one-of-a-kind teacher preparation program where undergraduates are trained to be teachers, as has been the case for its more than 200-year history, yet faculty are also heavily involved in research and graduate teaching. Among all U.S. universities ranked in the top twenty nationally by *U.S. News & World Report,* Vanderbilt is the only university where an undergraduate can be trained and certified to be an elementary or secondary teacher. In all other elite universities, a prospective teacher can become certified only after earning a bachelor's degree and enrolling in a master's of teaching program.

So, what does Peabody do with its unique blend of students and resources? Five things stand out:

- Intellectual model of instruction
- Practice and more practice
- Content and research knowledge
- Instructional rigor
- Accountability

AN INTELLECTUAL MODEL OF INSTRUCTION

They don't label it with academic jargon or give it a brand name. It's not constructivism or direct instruction. But in interviews with nine Peabody faculty members and administrators and nine students, a common approach to proper teaching was described by all. The term used most frequently was "intellectual." Peabody trains teachers to see instruction as an enterprise requiring an investment of substantial intelligence. It requires teachers to know their subject matter very well—on which more below. It requires teachers to know how students of different ages tend to think about different subjects. The director of early childhood education, Amy Palmeri, described how her own research in her specialty, science education, had identified consistent patterns of understanding and misconception that children typically bring to the study of science in the early years. Thus, science lessons must be planned in anticipation of that prior knowledge about, for example, the sun, the moon, and the seasons. The chair of the Department of Teaching and Learning, Rogers Hall, a computer science PhD recruited from the University of California–Berkeley and a specialist in math education, described a course that he delivers to future math teachers that helps them understand how students come to grasp math or misunderstand it. Among other things, his students study the work of William Schmidt from Michigan State University to better understand international approaches to math education and the different implications drawn from these studies for teaching in the U.S. context.[41]

The Peabody approach to teaching places heavy emphasis on teachers knowing where students stand at any given time. Formative assessment was emphasized by every student interviewed, and by most faculty as well. The point is a basic one. There is no such thing as teaching without learning. Successful teachers must know what their students know, don't know, are learning, and are not learning—all year long—to provide students the instruction they need. Peabody also emphasizes academic standards—they are the target of what teachers should be teaching. The standards include those set by the state of Tennessee (where Peabody teachers become certified). But teachers are trained to know standards beyond the sometimes minimal ones set by the states. Teachers are taught to aim high.

Teachers are prepared to work with a wide range of curricula. Peabody "trains teachers for the nation," as Dean Benbow puts it. Many graduates accept initial teaching positions in Tennessee schools, but Vanderbilt enrolls students from every state in the nation, and Peabody tries to prepare teachers to teach anywhere. Teachers may find themselves in school systems where a prescriptive reading or math program is required to be followed, or they may find themselves in systems where teachers are writing curriculum themselves. They may find themselves handed progressive published programs like so-called "fuzzy math" or back-to-the basics programs like Saxon Math. Peabody trains its teachers to understand the pros and cons of a range of instructional approaches and curricular materials and to use them "intelligently." Candidates develop skills for assessing how the published curricula match up with standards and with the needs of their students, and then employ or bolster curricula as needed to achieve student outcomes.

In one way or another, every teacher, however trained, has to bring all of these elements together in his or her teaching. The difference at Peabody is that it makes a virtue of the complexity and works with teachers until they master this demanding view of instruction. One of the very bright undergraduates interviewed said she appreciated Peabody because it recognized that "teaching is really hard." It's not a profession for students who don't want to work hard or who have no other options. It should be an affirmative choice for top students. Or as another student put it, she likes Peabody because "it treats teaching like the complex activity that it is." The chair of the Department of Teaching and Learning supported the students' views independently, saying, "Teaching must become a form of intellectual work or bright people will not do it." Peabody students have all of the options in the world; they will not choose or remain in teaching if it does not present a challenge.

PRACTICE, PRACTICE, PRACTICE

Teaching is not some sort of academic puzzle for students to contemplate in the abstract. Teaching is, in fact, complex. It needs to be understood as such, and then mastered on those terms. Peabody is committed to both the intellectual model and its execution. Lesser institutions may lecture students that teaching demands thought and reflection. But they fail to support the complexity with preparation for how to survive it in real classrooms. Hence the common criticism from recent education school graduates that they got too much theory and not enough practice.

Peabody's program is clinical from the start. For undergraduates, training in public school classrooms begins in the freshman year. It continues and grows each year through graduation four years later. The first year includes about twenty-five hours in schools, divided between observations and volunteer work. Commonly, courses include a mix of university and school-based work, more school-based with each passing year. In the sophomore year, the time in schools increases and the teaching candidate is assigned to work with an individual student. In the junior year, students have one practicum each semester, each mixing university instruction and school experience. For a future elementary teacher the fall might be devoted to a math/science block, the spring to reading/language arts. Senior year begins with another practicum, perhaps students with special needs. The year culminates with a full semester of student teaching, comprising two separate school placements.

Many features distinguish this program from norms nationwide. First, students spend a great deal of time in schools and classrooms. Peabody undergraduates log up to 800 hours of school time during their four years in the program. That is equivalent to one full year as a full-time school teacher. Typical teacher education programs offer little more than the obligatory semester of student teaching. Research is very clear that teachers become more effective in raising student achievement with classroom experience, at least for the first three or four years in the classroom.[42] Peabody is trying to provide prospective teachers that critical experience before they step into the classroom on their own. By stretching out a full year of classroom experiences over four years, Peabody gives candidates time to make mistakes, receive expert faculty feedback, try new things, and systematically learn from experience. Their 750–800 hours of school experience are likely to provide for more improvement than the baptism by fire that new teachers often count for their first 800 hours of experience.[43]

The clinical experience has other distinguishing qualities. Peabody works hard to ensure that its students have high-quality, school-based experiences. Select Peabody faculty take responsibility for student placement in local public schools. Receiving schools and teachers are hand-picked to provide individually useful matches. Teachers who will become mentors to student teachers are trained intensively—some during the summer on Peabody's campus and others in small groups at their schools. Peabody faculty explained that it is becoming harder and harder to find cooperative placements as schools become focused on meeting state student achievement goals. Student teaching may steal valuable time from teachers preparing students for standardized assessments. Peabody has addressed this concern by ensuring that its candidates are ready to deliver lessons that are aligned in substance and pacing with state and district content standards. Peabody's level of engagement with receiving schools is unusual, as a comparison with the findings of the recent study by the National Council on Teacher Quality (NCTQ) of student teaching readily reveals.[44]

Peabody faculty members are also heavily involved in the school-based experiences themselves. The Peabody undergraduate program is fairly small—60 graduates per year—and the ratio to faculty quite low.[45] Peabody is able to uphold the expectation that in practicum and student teaching, the students receive regular feedback and coaching from faculty. Students were effusive in their praise. Every student rated the field experience as one of the two most important elements of the Peabody experience. One stressed the "tight alignment between faculty member, mentor teacher, and student." Another commented that she "could not have asked for better placements; they were tailor-made for me" by her professor. As Benbow put it, "We craft our teachers one at a time." A good marketing tag line to be sure—but fundamental to the school's intensive coaching model, made possible by ample resources and small size, and confirmed as reality by all involved.

CONTENT KNOWLEDGE, RESEARCH KNOWLEDGE

Every undergraduate teaching candidate at Peabody must have a double major in an education field and a non-education field. A student majoring in secondary education must also have a major in the academic field in which the student aims to be certified, such as mathematics, biology, or English. A student majoring in elementary education or early childhood education must also hold a second non-education major, such as psychology or an academic subject.[46]

Many states now have a double major as a requirement for secondary teacher certification. And non-education majors are being required more frequently at all levels. These requirements may improve teacher effectiveness, as subject matter knowledge is a significant predictor of teacher quality at least in some subjects and at some grade levels.[47] But there is a difference between requiring a second major and putting that second major into serious use in a teacher education program. The director of secondary education, Barbara Stengel, stresses content knowledge as the hallmark of Peabody's program—"it's front and center." It's also taught to the highest level. Students acquire their content knowledge in an elite university, along with students who are seeking these majors for such demanding professions as medicine and engineering.

Reinforcing excellent content knowledge, Peabody includes some of the nation's leaders in math education, science education, reading instruction, and special education. They understand academic content. And they have researched extensively how students learn it and how teachers might most successfully teach it. There is an abiding respect for content knowledge and the criticality of teachers having command of it. Elementary teachers, for example, may not have to teach more than fifth grade math. But they need to know much more than fifth grade math to help their students appreciate mathematical reasoning, grasp more than rote algorithms, and understand why they might want to pursue and master math at advanced levels. As Benbow put it, "You can't teach something if you don't know it deeply."

Peabody researchers tend to be very focused on classrooms and students in their research. They bring to Peabody teaching candidates the latest that research has to offer in effective content instruction. Peabody students become very sensitive to the research basis for practices they may want to adopt in their own lessons. Palmeri recounted a student discussion last year of former TFA leader Doug Lemov's book, *Teach Like a Champion*. Students liked the book, found it persuasive and potentially helpful, but were all but in shock that the book had no research to back up its recommendations.

Students commented frequently on the integration of research with classroom practice. As one student said, "Peabody is very good at immersing you in research and combining that with what works in practice." The chairman of the Department of Special Education, Mark Wolery, put it this way: "We are committed to the view, supported by research, that special needs students learn content through purposeful direct instruction in that content. Our faculty's own research connects with interventions, students and classrooms. It is very focused on kids. New knowledge gets to our teaching candidates fast because they are very bright and faculty members are able to share with them readily." Students appreciate that Peabody professors are doing research that relates to instruction; they also appreciate that those professors are leaders at doing it. As a student put it, "We are very conscious that we are being taught by the very best."

INSTRUCTIONAL RIGOR

As much as Peabody's program is a "thinking person's model" of teacher education, it is also a model disciplined by structure. It is based, as just described, on a strong foundation of content knowledge. Its intellectual model of instruction is translated into practice through a highly specified model for individual lessons. Originated at Stanford University, the Teacher Performance Assessment (TPA) model has been refined at Peabody and is now used for lesson planning from early childhood through secondary education.[48]

Students develop model lessons before they ever enter a classroom to practice teaching on their own. The model is guided by a formal rubric for evaluating each lesson component. Faculty and students are often trained as "jurors" to provide consistent and reliable evaluations of lessons, component by component. Peabody does not follow the "know it when we see it" model of instruction; faculty specify it. Faculty also research components of the model, working to identify the right "grain size" of instructional elements that have consistent effects on achievement.

The framework employed at Peabody is similar to the new system used by the state of Tennessee for formal evaluations of teachers. The TPA is more rigorous, demanding that teachers analyze their own lessons as well as be observed. Several Peabody students interviewed are now teaching in Nashville public schools. While their colleagues are very anxious about the multiple observations they now face each year—veterans as well as beginners—the Peabody alumni are unfazed. They have trained on a similar system for four years. Students claim that school evaluators are not nearly as tough as the faculty who trained them.

To be sure, the framework employed at Peabody has a way to go before its impact on student achievement will be validated. Nationwide, research on similar frameworks, used at scale, is just beginning. It is unlikely, in the end, that any lesson plan will become the holy grail of instruction—leading every compliant teacher to the promised land of top quality performance. But teacher training also needs accepted best practices if teaching is to become less an art and more a science. Research along these lines is to be encouraged. Meanwhile, Peabody teachers have a consistent framework for guidance. The bottom line is that they are trained to be intellectual, thoughtful teachers.

ACCOUNTABILITY

Accountability came first to America's schools. Now it is coming to America's teachers. It is all based in the end on whether students learn. These are reasonable ideas to embrace in concept, but they have been controversial in practice. Educators in particular object to the measurement of learning with standardized test scores and to being held responsible for outcomes that are partly out of their control—influenced by families, peers, and the like. How does Peabody feel about these movements, and what has it done to accommodate them?

It is fair to say that Peabody has embraced the challenge. Peabody has an accountability culture of its own. For years, it has surveyed graduates of its teaching programs one, three, and five years after graduation. Peabody also surveys the principals supervising their graduates. Response rates are high— about 70 percent. Peabody tracks these data. It wants to know if teachers feel adequately prepared and, if not, in what areas the school could do a better job. It wants to know if teachers are staying with the profession. It wants to know what principals see as the strengths and weaknesses of Peabody's graduates.

Peabody has been pleased to find very high levels of satisfaction from its graduates and their employers—90 percent on average. Contrast this with the national survey by Levine and his team. Among principals, 62 percent agreed that schools of education did not prepare teachers well for the realities of teaching. Among teachers, 42 percent thought that they were not well-prepared across a range of teaching responsibilities.[49] Not all marks at Peabody over the years have been high. Several faculty members commented in interviews that surveys showed their teachers insufficiently prepared to work with the families of their students. The college subsequently worked to improve programming in that area.

Peabody has also embraced the testing movement for students and for teachers. Teacher preparation places heavy emphasis on data analysis. Prospective teachers are trained to disaggregate state test scores and to understand the needs of their new students and the successes and failures of their past students. They are schooled in formative assessments to track student progress throughout the school year. Peabody grads took state testing in stride, seeing it as a minimum standard that well-educated students should master. They had no problem incorporating test preparation into well-rounded lessons. They formed these opinions, moreover, in urban schools, in and around Nashville. Peabody students were taken aback by the pressure that schools and teachers now routinely experience. But they felt very well prepared for test-based accountability.

When it came to teacher accountability, views were much the same. Yes, there was griping among faculty about some of the "bugs" in Tennessee's system—such as scoring the added value of elementary music, art, physical education, and K–2 teachers using the scores of teachers in grades 3–5. There was also concern with the ways data are being used once value-added scores are obtained. But faculty members accept the concept when part of a balanced system of teacher evaluation. They recognize the importance of preparing teachers to teach to the highest standards while also succeeding by more limited value-added measures. Faculty were proud that Vanderbilt graduates were proving themselves effective in state evaluations.

TRAINING THE BEST?

The evidence is overwhelming. The United States attracts students into teacher preparation programs who are average at best, and then trains them in colleges and universities that are below par for the nation and in education programs that are weak in faculty and design. Those programs produce teachers who yield below-average student results. There is little disagreement—except perhaps from the sub-par institutions themselves—that this is a bad plan for preparing U.S. teachers. It is ludicrous if the United States seriously wants the best teachers in the world.

The evidence is also clear. Teachers are the single strongest school-based influence on the achievement of students. With annual testing of students and integrated databases, states can measure the added value of most teachers and use that information to retain the most successful.

But what of the rest? Improve them? Remove them? Research is unclear how teachers can be improved. Research is also unclear about how to hire promising teachers to replace those who might be removed.

But the issue is not opaque either. Academically strong teachers are more successful than academically weak teachers. Academically strong institutions appear to do a better job preparing teachers to raise achievement than academically weak institutions. Successful teaching is an inherently complex job—done right, it is intellectually demanding. Teachers get better at it through experience, at least in the early going. Strong teacher preparation programs can capitalize on the need for experience by building clinical training programs that carefully coach budding teachers through well-designed school-based experiences.

The success of both Peabody and Teach for America raises the important question of how much teacher effectiveness hinges on the aptitude of the teacher and how much on the quality of the teacher preparation. Both programs have evidence of producing teachers who raise achievement significantly more than the average. Obviously, the two programs take very different approaches to teacher preparation. But it may not be necessary for the nation's policymakers to choose between the two approaches. TFA would never argue that demanding preparation and strong on-the-job support are unnecessary, or that smart young people can succeed in classrooms on the basis of wits alone. TFA simply represents a different approach to identifying top teaching prospects and then helping them learn the craft.

Peabody illustrates what a well-balanced pre-service training program might include: an intellectual model of teaching, a full year's worth of closely supervised school-based practice, a foundation of strong subject matter expertise, faculty connected to schools through experience and research, systematic guides to best classroom practice, and a focus on student outcomes. The evidence is that this model works.

The model works with exceptionally bright students. In interviews with Peabody faculty and students, everyone was asked if the Peabody model could work with students of less aptitude or achievement. Students, hesitant to acknowledge their own academic gifts, emphasized the importance of other teacher attributes such as passion, perseverance, and a love for children. Faculty members were more reflective. While they too recognized the non-cognitive attributes that successful teachers must have, they also emphasized that teaching was not for below-average folk. SAT scores need not be 1400, but they cannot be 1000—or lower—either.

If America truly wants the best teachers in the world, it must attract and retain individuals with higher academic potential. If it wants them to succeed at high rates in the classroom, it should look to training programs that provide extensive clinical experience and academic rigor. America's doctoral universities are the best bet to fill that bill. But so too may be alternative programs such as TFA or The New Teacher Project, perhaps affiliated with research universities. Master's universities and baccalaureate colleges may be able to do the job as well. But for most of them, success will require major changes.

There are also the matters of cost and scale. Elite universities and colleges like Vanderbilt are expensive—over $55,000 per year all-in. Teachers prepared in such institutions are receiving far more than a teacher-preparation program; they are gaining an academically rigorous undergraduate education. Teach for America is infinitely cheaper if viewed only as a teacher preparation program. Five weeks of summer training and ongoing support are a fraction of the cost of a four-year degree at an elite institution. But this is a misleading comparison. TFA candidates are almost all graduates of top colleges and universities, with hefty price tags. Master's universities, the traditional training ground of most teachers, are cheaper than both alternatives, often being public institutions with state subsidies. But, what are the subsidies buying? If it is ineffective teacher education, what is the value in that?

As a practical matter, the United States will also require large numbers of teachers—far more than elite institutions could ever provide. Even if public schools employ only 2.5 million teachers, and if annual turnover drops to 5 percent, over 100,000 new teachers will be required each year. If the top 300 universities and colleges in the country (roughly all of those with average freshman SAT scores above 1000) each produced 300 teachers a year, that would still not be enough. And that is a stretch, in any case, as most of these institutions currently produce far fewer than 300 teachers per year. The United States clearly needs alternative programs like Teach for America. It may also need colleges and universities that currently serve students of below-average academic ability and produce teachers with below-average rates of success—the bulk of traditional schools of education.

This could be an unhappy prospect, counting on alternatives that do not now exist in sufficient number or accepting options known not to work. But policymakers do not have to make such unpleasant choices. Policymakers should provide strong incentives for training programs of all types to improve. The programs that are wanting today could and should become better programs tomorrow. Policymakers should also provide strong incentives for teachers and employers to patronize the programs that work best. Prospective teachers can evaluate the costs of training programs against the benefits. Policymakers can decide how to subsidize, with grants and loans, prospective teachers who cannot afford the best options. Policymakers can also decide how to subsidize training programs directly, knowing the costs and, most important, the benefits.

The key to all of this is *data*. America's teachers should be trained in those institutions that demonstrate that they can prepare teachers who can help students achieve high academic standards. Policymakers should focus on acquiring the data necessary to evaluate the effectiveness of training programs of all kinds, and then making sure those data are in the hands of prospective teachers, high school guidance counselors, school districts, and building principals. Policymakers should not be mandating where and how teachers are trained. They should be ensuring that the people with the most interest in quality training have the knowledge and incentive to support what works. The next chapter explains how.

CHAPTER 4

Great Leaders, Great Teachers

In an alternative world, teacher quality would not be such a problem. Teachers would be hired through an evaluation of formal credentials, work history, and performance during the interview process. Once on the job, teachers would be observed, coached, and evaluated. Some would be judged successes and rewarded with compensation or additional responsibility, such as coaching new teachers. Others would be judged unsuccessful and be encouraged or asked to leave. Performance would be gauged by some combination of objective and subjective factors. These actions and decisions would be taken by skilled managers held accountable for doing them well.

This is how talent development works in other professions and industries where individual performance is difficult to predict and measure, but crucial to the overall success of the organization.[1] Managers are equipped, to whatever extent possible, with formal tools of evaluation, and employees are given appropriate incentives to perform. But in the end, the manager closest to the job is responsible for judging and developing talent and is rewarded for doing so. Indeed, this is the manager's most important role—getting the best people possible in their respective positions and helping them to perform.[2]

In schools, the manager's role would fall to the principal. He or she would be responsible for identifying prospective teachers with the potential to develop into effective instructors and good team members; for building a school organization where teachers have maximum opportunity to learn and improve; for recruiting and retaining veteran teachers who can get great results for students and help other teachers improve; for creating work conditions where quality teachers want to remain; and for making the tough decisions to remove unsuccessful teachers from the school. School districts could help principals in this role with evaluation tools and data. But the job of ensuring teacher quality would ultimately be the job of the principal.

If principals were actually able to perform this role, the problem of teacher quality would become quite different. It would become a fraction of the size. It would become less a problem of finding 3 million great teachers to lead America's classrooms and more a problem of finding 90,000 great principals to lead America's schools. These tasks are interdependent, of course, and policymakers must give careful thought to the conditions that will attract and keep high-caliber performers in teaching—and make the principal's job that much easier. The teacher quality challenge does not quite reduce to just 90,000 principals. But if principals can in fact deliver on teacher quality, the problem does become more tractable. The evidence is they can. The problem is most principals have not.

From Teachers to Leaders

In 1994, two young teachers, fresh out of service to Teach for America, started a fifth-grade school program in inner city Houston, Texas.[3] Working with forty-eight low-income students, half of whom had failed their state assessments the year prior, and emphasizing high expectations and relentless hard work, Mike Feinberg and David Levin helped 98 percent pass the state assessments in both reading and math by year's end. In a story that is now legend, the two called their approach the Knowledge is Power Program—or KIPP—and proceeded to open two small schools the next year. Feinberg ran the KIPP Academy Middle School in Houston and Levin returned home to New York to open KIPP Academy in the South Bronx.

The schools were founded on what Feinberg and Levin called their Five Pillars:

- High Expectations: KIPP schools have clearly defined and measurable high expectations for academic achievement and conduct.
- Choice and Commitment: Students, their parents, and the faculty of each KIPP school choose to participate in the program. Everyone must make and uphold a commitment to the school and to each other to put in the time and effort to achieve success.
- More Time: With an extended day, week, and year, students have more time in the classroom to acquire the academic knowledge and skills that will prepare them for college.
- Power to Lead: Principals have control over the school budget and personnel allowing them maximum effectiveness in helping students learn.
- Focus on Results: KIPP schools relentlessly focus on student performance and character development.

Though Feinberg and Levin were not explicit about it at this early stage, the pillars elevated the role of school leadership. In public schools, principals seldom have control over their entire budgets, nor do they have free rein to hire and fire teachers and other school staff. Feinberg and Levin insisted that principals of KIPP schools have this authority. Schools, like any organization that hopes to succeed, need absolute clarity about goals and they need measures of progress. It is the leader's job—the principal's job—to establish them and keep the organization totally focused on them. In KIPP schools, Feinberg and Levin wanted the principal to make high achievement and strong character everyone's priority. They also wanted KIPP schools to ensure that no one—staff or student—was there involuntarily. Teachers would not be assigned to KIPP schools by district offices; principals would build their own teams. Strong leaders do.

Feinberg and Levin approached the creation of KIPP schools as great teachers. They learned from their own efforts as teachers about what it takes to help every student succeed. Time, they discovered, is crucial. Many students, particularly from disadvantaged homes, simply cannot master the knowledge and skills required at each grade level in the time allotted. Schools and teachers must be willing to put in the necessary time and not be tied to a traditional school day or year. And, students need whatever help their families can offer. So Feinberg and Levin asked that families choose KIPP and sign commitments to support their students. Feinberg and Levin also saw the power of students believing in themselves, something teachers could inspire and inculcate by preaching and teaching high expectations and promising college for all.

As Feinberg and Levin transitioned from full-time teachers to leaders, they took the lessons that they learned as teachers and applied them school-wide. They then vested in the principal—the role each now assumed—power and responsibility to make the lessons learned in their own classrooms apply to all classrooms. They were teacher-leaders—with a firm grasp of the levers that principals need to make vision reality.

Over the next several years, Feinberg and Levin achieved outstanding results with increasing numbers of students. Their success caught the eye of the media and reformers. In 2000 Feinberg and Levin were approached by Doris and Don Fisher, the founders of Gap Inc., about the possibility of replicating the success of the early KIPP schools. The Fishers donated the initial funds to launch the KIPP Foundation, and the replication process began. Today there are 109 KIPP schools in twenty states and the District of Columbia. KIPP has expanded beyond its original focus on middle schools to now include thirty elementary schools, sixty-one middle schools, and eighteen high schools. The network of schools serves 32,000 students.

Most important, the schools have maintained the high quality that first brought them notice. It is fair to say that KIPP schools represent the single most successful large-scale program for educating disadvantaged students in the United States over the last twenty years. Quality schools, of any type, have proven very difficult to replicate or take to appreciable scale. The nation is marked by countless isolated models of excellence. None has scaled with anything approaching the success of KIPP. Its replication strategy is deceptively simple: replicate great KIPP leaders and let them replicate the schools.

A TOP QUARTILE TEACHER IN EVERY CLASSROOM

It is worth considering closely the magnitude of KIPP's success. Research has now provided consistent evidence of the difference that great teachers can make for student achievement. How do the effects of KIPP schools compare? After all, KIPP schools employ nearly 2,000 teachers. Is KIPP somehow better able than most schools to attract, develop, and retain high-quality teachers in most classrooms? Or do KIPP schools suffer, like most schools, from variations in teacher quality that reduce the overall effectiveness of their schools?

Since KIPP first began making news with its success, questions have been raised about the program's effectiveness. Critics asked whether the commitment that KIPP extracts from every family seeking to enroll a student might discourage the most challenging students from joining KIPP schools. Others worried that the longer school day and year might discourage the most difficult students from enrolling, or lead them to drop out after giving the school a try. Several studies tried to address these issues while gauging KIPP's impact on student achievement. None was able to resolve issues of student selectivity fully. But each provided evidence that students in KIPP schools were achieving at higher rates than comparable students in traditional public schools.[4]

In 2010 a comprehensive long-term analysis of KIPP schools better satisfied concerns about selectivity—and produced eye-popping results. Mathematica, a distinguished independent social science research organization, analyzed twenty-two KIPP middle schools, the full population of KIPP schools for which test scores were available for at least four years. Although its methods were non-experimental—students randomly selected in lotteries to attend KIPP schools are not compared to students who applied to KIPP schools but were not selected in lotteries—the study took numerous measures to limit and test for selectivity bias. The study compared students in KIPP schools to comparable students in comparable public schools, using a procedure known as propensity matching. A follow-up study by Mathematica will compare results from a subset of KIPP schools that are over-subscribed and therefore filled via lottery.[5]

The long-term achievement effects in the twenty-two KIPP middle schools are remarkable for their size and their consistency. In mathematics, the one-year effect sizes ranged across KIPP schools from −0.1 to 0.75, with an average of approximately 0.3. The three-year effect sizes ranged from 0 to 0.8, with an average of roughly 0.5. An effect size of 0.4 after three years translates into an additional year of learning—a lot of extra value for that span of time. For perspective, the black-white achievement gap in the United States at fourth and eighth grades is about one standard deviation.[6] The benefits of KIPP schools could cut that gap in half, in math, in just three years.

In reading, the one-year effect sizes ranged across schools from −0.15 to 0.4, with an average of about 0.1. The three-year effect sizes in reading ranged from −0.1 to 0.9, with an average of around 0.25. After three years, an effect size of .31 is equivalent to one extra year of learning. KIPP schools average about 0.8 years of extra learning in reading.

The results are also highly consistent. In math, seventeen KIPP schools had positive effects after one year, fifteen of which were statistically significant. After three years, every school but one was positive and eighteen were statistically significant. In reading, seventeen KIPP schools were also positive after one year, though only eight were statistically significant. After three years, all but three KIPP schools were positive and fourteen were statistically significant. After three years, not a single KIPP school performed significantly worse than comparable public schools.

In the context of research on teacher quality, these results take on even greater significance. Recall that effect sizes for teacher quality are on the order of 0.1 to 0.2. In one year, changing a student from an average teacher (at the 50th percentile of the teacher effectiveness distribution) to a teacher one standard deviation above average (at the 84th percentile) will increase student achievement by 0.1 to 0.2 standard deviations. This is the largest known one-year effect on achievement of any single school-based factor. It is easy to imagine the consequences being even larger. If a student could switch from a teacher in the lowest quartile of performance to the highest quartile, the achievement gain could be 0.3 standard deviations. If that trade-up in quality could be repeated three years in a row, the achievement gains have been shown to accumulate, reaching as much as 0.5 standard deviations.

What KIPP has achieved is roughly comparable to having a top quartile teacher in every classroom in its schools. It is not unreasonable to infer that this is precisely how KIPP achieves its results. KIPP schools are distinguished by strong cultures designed to provide positive antidotes to the often negative influences of high poverty environments. KIPP schools exude high expectations for students. Day in and day out, students are instructed morally as well as academically. They are taught to "work hard and be nice."[7] They are told that they *will* go to college—every one of them. They are taught how to behave and how to learn, consistently from classroom to classroom. They learn there are no excuses.

All of these school-wide influences promote student commitment, engagement, and hard work. But, at the end of the day, every teacher is part of creating these conditions. KIPP cultures are powerful because they are replicated across every classroom in the school. Individual teachers must do this. Individual teachers must also teach. The state assessments do not measure commitment or hard work or aspirations. Assessments gauge reading and math skills and knowledge. It is the teachers—and really no one else—who ensure that students acquire the necessary knowledge and skills. Great teachers in any school have to learn how to motivate, engage, and manage their students. KIPP teachers have the benefit of working within a strong system that both provides them a model of classroom values and deportment and reinforces it school-wide. But teachers at KIPP must still execute the model successfully in their classrooms—and teach.

PROVING THE POSSIBLE

So, how does KIPP extract such high levels of performance from its teachers? In a word: leadership. KIPP schools were founded by two outstanding teachers. As they looked to repeat their own success, all they knew was getting more teachers to perform like them—to believe absolutely in every student's potential, to motivate with high expectations, to teach hard and long until every student gets it. The principal's job was to find and develop and hold accountable more and more teachers who were willing to do what the founders knew would work—and perhaps contribute to it over time.

As Feinberg and Levin confronted the challenge of replicating KIPP schools, they focused on developing principals who first and foremost could develop and manage high-performing teachers. KIPP has now evolved a formal Leadership Competency Model that drives everything that KIPP does to develop and manage its principals.[8] The core of the model has been unchanged since Feinberg and Levin conceived it. A principal's first job is to "prove the possible."

As Richard Barth, KIPP Foundation CEO, put it, "Great leaders begin as great teachers; that is the best bet, in our experience. KIPP teachers know that the principal knows how to do it. Principals have done it themselves and teachers see this." This is precisely what Feinberg and Levin meant when they said that the core of being a principal is "proving the possible." Principals lead by example. They have successfully taught in challenging communities. They have helped students with great disadvantages achieve high standards. They are not asking teachers to do anything that they would not, or could not, do themselves.

In the beginning, Feinberg and Levin were satisfied that "proving the possible" and just one other element defined successful leadership. Leaders needed to "drive results." As Barth described it, "Principals need to wake up every morning to make a difference in kids' lives." They need to be all but consumed with student achievement. There is nothing more important at school than ensuring student success. Everything that the principal does needs to be about achievement. The Competency Model explicates this. The principal needs to think critically, solve problems, make decisions, plan, and execute, all with a complete focus on achievement.

This way of thinking about the principal is far removed from traditional models of school leadership. It was once said that principals were about the "Bs:" buses, buildings, bells, budgets, and behavior. Principals need to make sure that schools operate smoothly and safely. Students must arrive and depart fully accounted for. A teacher must be in every classroom, and students need to be scheduled for instruction every minute of the day. Students must follow the rules and conduct themselves in class and between classes in ways that do not interfere with learning.

Programs that prepare principals for licensure in the United States certainly include instructional leadership as well as school management. In fact, instructional leadership is now the mantra of teacher preparation programs. A recent international study of school leadership by McKinsey urged nations to make instruction a much greater focus of principal preparation.[9] But it is a very different thing to make instruction a larger part of administrative training than it is to say that achievement is essentially all that matters. This is where KIPP's model of leadership is distinct. In the beginning Feinberg and Levin did not even pause to mention the administrative elements of being a principal. To them the job was all about teaching and results.

With time, the Leadership Competency Framework was rounded out with two additional elements. As Barth explained, KIPP found that its top leadership candidates "would go through a wall for kids—and through a teacher for kids." This kind of passion and commitment "cannot be taught." It is what KIPP is looking for in its principals. But, principals also need to know how to support and develop teachers as well. They can't just "go through them" if they aren't having immediate success. New teachers are not going to be able to teach like superstars right off the bat. As Barth said, "Teachers are not born, they are made." KIPP had to work hard to train aspiring principals in how to develop teachers, bring teachers together into a cohesive team, and plan collectively for the school's success. "Managing people" became the Framework's third major element.

Principals tended to have one other glaring deficit. In their laser-like focus on students and what was happening in their schools, they would often lose sight of the important stakeholders around them. Schools are not islands. They are surrounded by communities, families, school boards, media, and more. Their job is that much harder if they do not have external support. Families do not know what it takes to achieve at the levels KIPP is aiming for and need great assistance from the school if they are going to help. Communities may not embrace schools like KIPP, which can seem threatening to traditional public schools. Boards may not understand the tough policies that KIPP implements to ensure student commitment. The media can spread good will or bad about the school, depending on who is providing them information. KIPP added a fourth and final element to its Competency Framework— "building relationships."

SCALING LEADERSHIP

Today, the KIPP Foundation operates a five-tier system of leadership development that is the heart of its school replication strategy. The beginning tier is a one-year program for teachers who are becoming grade-level teacher chairs. They are trained in skills such as analyzing data, adapting instruction, and leading team meetings. These teacher leaders help to develop newer faculty and craft grade-level plans for student success. Many non-KIPP schools employ teacher teams to help distribute school leadership, but evidence indicates few provide adequate training for teacher leaders.

Next up the ladder is a one-year program for assistant principals. In KIPP schools, teacher leaders are groomed for school-wide leadership, which—if they pass muster—begins with promotion to assistant principal. Once in the role, new assistant principals join an intensive program that includes a summer institute, ongoing leadership workshops, and master's degree and credentialing programs. KIPP believes deeply in growing talent from within. Successful KIPP teachers know the model and the culture better than anyone. They can learn and develop the requisite leadership skills best by being coached on the job. They are not asked to acquire an administrative license before being eligible to become an assistant principal. Actually it is the reverse: they are assisted with their master's degree and credential *after* they demonstrate the potential to succeed as a KIPP principal.

For assistant principals who demonstrate the capacity to lead schools on their own, KIPP has a third program. The "successor principal program" begins with a summer institute and includes ongoing leadership workshops throughout the school year. It adds intensive coaching, a school review, and a residency—learning from another successful KIPP principal—to the regimen. Candidates are also helped, if necessary, with a master's degree program and credential. Successful participants in the demanding program are then placed in *existing* KIPP schools within eighteen months.

KIPP is regularly opening new schools. Those require an even higher level of preparation. For non-KIPP principals, the process takes two full years and is incredibly demanding and competitive. The first year is the Miles Family Fellowship for school founders. Non-KIPP leaders who aspire to open new KIPP schools must succeed in the keen competition for a Miles Family Fellowship and then prove in a grueling year of training that they deserve to go forward in a second year. Miles Fellows participate in a summer institute and ongoing leadership work-shops. Most important, they are custom-placed in a KIPP school that best fits their leadership needs and new school aspirations. They work through an individualized leadership development plan meant to hone the skills that most need improvement.

Founding principals, whether from the Miles program or KIPP schools, must then win the coveted Fisher Fellowship for founding principals. This program originated with the involve-ment of Doris and Don Fisher in 2000 and has become an exemplar of serious principal preparation ever since. After six weeks of summer training, the future principal is again placed in a KIPP school for at-elbow training by a high-performing KIPP principal. The placements are complemented with coach-ing and school reviews to ensure the future founder has the skills to be granted the privilege of opening a new KIPP school. The training and oversight are intense.

But nothing compares to the scrutiny given applicants for the Fisher Fellowship. Each year about 300 applicants are win-nowed to twenty Fellows. Applicants must prove they have sub-stantially raised student achievement. They must show that they can teach superbly themselves. The semi-finalists are subjected to what Barth describes as "multi-day grilling" on the four leadership competencies. In the end, Mike Feinberg himself helps select the Fellows.

This kind of commitment to leadership development is literally unheard of in public or private education. Every principal of a KIPP school—existing or new—has been through two or three years of training dedicated expressly to becoming a leader of the KIPP mold. The norm in public schools is for assistant principals to be appointed—green—after gaining administrative licensure *outside* of the school system. Principals are often appointed the same way, especially at the elementary level. Or, they are promoted from the ranks of assistant principals. School districts often have leadership development programs of some sort. But they tend to be brief, generic, and, with few exceptions, inconsequential.[10]

This is not surprising. The KIPP program is expensive. Fellows must be supported while they are not serving or being paid as full-time teachers or administrators. KIPP invests $150,000 alone in each founding principal. Assistant principals are uneconomical in small schools, but KIPP insists upon having them. The KIPP Foundation has raised $150 million in philanthropy since its inception, much of it to pay for its leadership development programs. From 2007–2010 KIPP trained nearly 400 current or aspiring principals.

In 2010 the U.S. Department of Education awarded KIPP a $50 million Investing in Innovation (i3) grant to take its leadership programs to a much larger scale. Over the grant period KIPP will train 1,000 school leaders. KIPP will double its rate of new KIPP school openings to eighteen per year. By 2020 KIPP projects to be serving 90,000 students—triple the current number. KIPP is also committed to offering its leadership development ideas and programs to public school districts. If KIPP has developed the proverbial "secret sauce" for preparing principals to run schools that raise achievement, perhaps public schools can follow the recipe and enjoy similar success. Perhaps—but not likely.

Why So Few Great Principals?

KIPP has not really invented a secret sauce. What KIPP has done is to take dead-seriously the ideas that research has been validating for quite some time. As early as 1980, researchers had identified highly effective schools in which principals seemed to play vital roles. These schools were beating the odds, helping students achieve when their families and peer groups predicted they would not. These schools seemed to share certain attributes: a sharp focus on academics, high expectations for student achievement, palpably positive cultures, collaborative teachers, and strong principals. Specifically, they had principals who provided a vision of what was possible, pulled teachers together into committed teams, and did whatever was necessary to achieve results . . . a lot like KIPP principals today.[11]

In the years since, research as well as reform has pointed to principal leadership as a key to student achievement. The McKinsey study, referenced above, argued that "school leadership is second only to classroom teaching as an influence on student learning."[12] It quoted with approval the conclusion of the British school inspectorate that "93 percent of schools with strong leadership have strong achievement." It went on to highlight principal development programs in eight successful school systems around the world. The study argued that principal development must place much more emphasis on the instructional elements of the job and not those traditional Bs.

Robert Marzano, a researcher influential in public school circles, helped produce a meta-analysis of principal leadership.[13] Summarizing seventy high-quality studies, Marzano and team

found an average effect size of leadership on student achievement of 0.25. It found twenty-one statistically significant dimensions of effective principal leadership—such things as culture,
order, discipline, focus, knowledge of curriculum and instruction, visibility, communication, and contingent rewards. The
study recommended a program of "balanced leadership" to prepare principals for the demanding job. Principals could make
a major difference in student achievement if they embraced the
need to lead and not just manage. More recent research by
Rick Hess of the American Enterprise Institute supports this
recommendation.[14]

Public schools have certainly heard these messages. Principal
development and appraisal frameworks now commonly include
expectations that principals provide instructional leadership,
promote staff development, and build effective teams. No one in
public education would dispute the need for principals to be
more like those recommended by McKinsey, Marzano and team,
or hundreds of other contemporary models of school leadership.
The sauce is not a secret, and everyone says that they like it.

Yet, there are not many highly effective principals. Achievement in U.S. schools is well below standards that anyone finds
acceptable. If principals have such a large impact on student
achievement, clearly many principals are not doing a stellar job.
The United States cannot have both high percentages of great
principals and high percentages of poor schools. While there
are no data to compare and evaluate objectively all of America's
principals, it is fair to say that there are not nearly enough truly
good ones. Student achievement would not be the problem that
it is, if great principals were the norm.

Great principals are likely to be much more difficult to develop
than school reformers like McKinsey, Marzano, and other popular authorities suggest. The reasons are absolutely fundamental.
First, the best evidence is that the most important role that prin-

cipals play in driving student achievement is ensuring a school full of top-notch teachers. If principals are not successful in this task, they will not be successful in raising student achievement—full stop. This is also the hardest assignment that principals face. It is hard in its own right, but harder still for the second reason that discourages strong school leaders: public education is not generally structured to attract and promote principals who are truly strong. It is more accurate to say public education is structured to discourage strong leadership. It is no accident that KIPP's leaders have been developed outside traditional structures.

IT'S ALL ABOUT THE TEACHERS

Principal leadership has been the subject of countless studies, many qualitative—highlighting the behavior of unusually successful principals—but many quantitative, too. As Marzano and team helpfully summarize, numerous studies have found statistically significant relationships between particular principal behaviors and student achievement. The number and variety of findings surely indicate that principals with positive attributes tend to lead schools that raise student achievement. But the studies also raise the vital question: how? How does a principal's knowledge of curriculum and instruction, for example, raise the test scores of students? How does the principal's skill in building culture improve math achievement? How does the principal's use of contingent rewards boost reading comprehension?

The reality is that most research that touts the influence of the principal does not explain how that influence affects the student. Most research also fails to separate the influence of the principal from that of the teachers who are actually working with the students. If the effectiveness of teachers were figured into the equation, it is likely that the independent influence of the principal would attenuate or disappear altogether. The best guess about principal effectiveness is that it largely works through the teachers. There may well be twenty-one individual skills that effective principals demonstrate. But those skills matter for students because they promote the effectiveness of teachers.

Recent research has begun to validate this line of reasoning. Economists responsible for providing robust estimates of teacher effectiveness have now turned their attention to principals. They have found remarkably strong principal effects on student achievement. Effect sizes may be as large as 0.26, but no smaller than 0.05–0.10 and statistically significant.[15] These effect sizes are on the order of those established for individual teachers. But the effects of principals apply school-wide and not just to an individual classroom. Important as well, the effect sizes are greatest for schools with the highest levels of poverty. Changing leadership from a bottom quartile principal to a top quartile principal can make a sizable difference in achievement for America's most disadvantaged schools.

This same research has also begun to ask the million-dollar question: what is it that these principals do that enables them to raise achievement? The answer, as best these data can reveal, is that successful principals are especially effective at ridding their schools of highly ineffective teachers and at retaining highly effective teachers. The higher the quality of the principal, as measured by value added to achievement, the more net teacher turnover is associated with rising value-added scores among teachers. The relationship is particularly strong among top quartile principals.[16]

The data that make it possible to gauge principal and teacher effects on achievement have become available only in recent years. Only a small number of states have enough years of data to allow reliable estimates of these effects. As with teacher effects, research on principal effects must first establish their magnitude and then explain them. Teacher effects are well established—and large. They are not yet well understood. Principal effects seem to be large as well. But they may be closer to being understood.

Logic alone suggests that the influence of principals on student achievement occurs through the influence of teachers. Principals do not teach students directly. Principals help set the tone of the building in which students learn and help establish positive discipline. These and other contributions make a school a more (or less) attractive place to learn. But even these indirect influences on learning would be nothing if not carried out by the teachers. Obviously, academic instruction, no matter how carefully planned or monitored by the principal, must be delivered by the teachers. It stands to reason that the effect of the principal may occur largely through the performance of the teaching staff that the principal selects, develops, motivates, retains, deselects, and sometimes loses.

There is also considerable evidence to support this reasoning. It is very well established that principals are one of the most important determinants of teacher turnover.[17] For years, policymakers have been concerned about the poor rate of retention of new teachers in the profession. Roughly one in five newly minted teachers leave the profession within five years of beginning. Teachers also turn over at high rates in schools with high levels of poverty. There is some evidence that the teachers leaving the profession or leaving the toughest schools may be teachers of relatively high potential.[18] Turnover, in other words, is not a positive. Research has established that working conditions in schools are the number one cause of turnover. Principals are largely responsible for establishing working conditions. Research has also demonstrated that teacher turnover is highest in schools with the least effective principals, regardless of poverty.[19] Principals are crucial in determining which teachers remain voluntarily in their schools.

Principals also have the ability to discern which teachers ought to remain on staff and which teachers ought to be asked or encouraged to leave. A recent study showed that principals are very good at judging the value-added achievement of their teachers. This is important. It's one thing for a principal to know which teachers have students obtaining high or low test scores or making gains year on year. But it is quite another level of sophistication for principals to be able to judge which teachers add value to test scores after controlling for the other factors that cause scores to rise or fall. Principals are especially adept at identifying their lowest and highest quartile teachers.[20]

Tools are now being honed to help principals make these judgments more expertly. Charlotte Danielson, formerly with the Educational Testing Service and an author of Praxis exams, has developed a tool for observing and measuring teacher behaviors linked to student achievement. Her Framework for Teaching (FFT) employs eight dimensions of instruction, such as engaging students, using assessment in instruction, and discussion and questioning techniques, to rate teachers on a four-point, detailed rubric ranging from unsatisfactory to basic to proficient to distinguished. Researchers at the University of Virginia have developed a similar tool, the Classroom Assessment Scoring System (CLASS).

Recently, economists Thomas Kane and Douglas Staiger, leaders in the analysis of teacher effectiveness, led a project that tested the ability of FFT, CLASS, and three other frameworks to produce reliable and valid assessments of teacher effectiveness.[21] Principals and teachers were trained online in the use of the tools. They then evaluated some 7,000 videotaped lessons from real-life classrooms and teachers, several lessons per teacher. They found that the tools produced reliable scores at the level of individual teachers. More important, they found that the observation-based average scores for individual teachers were strong predictors of the achievement of the teachers' students. These observation-based scores coupled with value-added scores from teachers' previous years of instruction were very strong predictors—with each predictor statistically significant.

In short, research is demonstrating that principals *can* judge teacher effectiveness accurately. If principals were equipped in the future with test-based value-added scores and with observation-based measures of instruction, they would be well-equipped to judge which teachers could benefit from additional development, which ones were superstars who had to be retained, and which ones perhaps needed to move on. With the Obama administration's encouragement, through its ESEA waiver process and Race to the Top grant competition, states are now overhauling teacher evaluation systems to include value-added and observational elements. The qualitative element typically involves observations by mentors and peers as well as principals. An advantage of multiple observers is that it makes it possible to calibrate the quality of each judge and to retrain them if necessary. Authorities could ensure, in other words, that principals are effective judges of teacher talent.[22]

So, we know that the best principals improve teacher effectiveness by retaining top performers and losing bottom performers. We know that principals shape the working conditions that are a leading cause of teacher retention or turnover. We know that ineffective principals spur turnover, regardless of poverty. We know that principals are good judges of teacher talent, and could be even better. Effective principals clearly gain some of their effectiveness by determining who teaches on their staffs. This is a powerful source of influence over achievement, as the teachers are the ones who actually do the teaching.

There is one additional reason to believe that principals exert their influence over achievement through their teachers. That is the role that principals play in teacher development. Research has shown that effective teachers are difficult to pick out based on their resumes. The most comprehensive study to date estimates that principals could improve their selection of new teachers by an effect size of 0.03 if they employed a combination of objective measures of cognitive and non-cognitive ability.[23] Principals *should* consider the aptitude, for example, of new teachers. But, most of the success of new teachers will be determined on the job. Research has very firmly established that teachers gain effectiveness with experience.[24] But, not all teachers become effective with experience. Indeed, research has shown that teachers ultimately vary widely in effectiveness.

Principals have a lot to do with whether teachers learn from experience. There is little evidence that teachers benefit from district-provided professional development programs.[25] It appears rather that teachers improve through experience, shaped by support and feedback from teachers and leaders in the school. Principals have much to do with whether teachers have helpful experiences. Principals obviously determine the caliber of teachers from whom rookies learn; they shape the school staff. Principals also organize the school, its team structure, its opportunities for teachers to plan and work together, its use of formal mentoring, and most anything else that might offer teachers support.

KIPP provides a great example of this. KIPP has two gatekeeping standards for its principals: have they produced high levels of achievement themselves—as a teacher, assistant principal, or non-KIPP principal—and can they teach? For KIPP, the principal's job is first and foremost about quality teaching and results for kids. Principals need to know how to produce both. Barth attributes principal success to a "developmental mindset." KIPP trains principals how to *hire* teachers, empha-sizing evidence of prior success in raising student achievement. But Barth allows that KIPP is "imperfect" at hiring.

Principals succeed, Barth said, by "getting everyone aligned around mission and vision"—building the KIPP culture. But the key to principal success is "they are amazing at growing talent and helping people become better teachers." KIPP principals are "in classes all the time, giving feedback, developing teacher lead-ers, and creating a culture of continuous improvement." KIPP principals are supportive. KIPP principals are also tough. As Barth put it, "the best leaders are truth tellers; they do not pull their punches." He added that KIPP principals "are comfortable holding adults accountable." The combination of intelligent sup-port and uncompromising accountability—what might be called tough love—obviously works for KIPP principals.

It also works elsewhere. San Jose Charter Academy, the high-performing low-income school introduced in chapter 2, has much more going for it than innovative technology. Its 300-point ascent of the state accountability scale occurred the old-fashioned way, through determined and successful class-room teaching. Denise Patton, the only principal the school has ever had—now in her thirteenth year—knows a thing or two about leadership. Asked what role is most important for producing substantial and long-lasting achievement gains, she credited "filling the classrooms with the best teachers possible, teachers who are totally focused on students."

How does Patton do this? She had eight years of experience teaching before she became principal and knows good instruc-tion. She tries to hire well. She said, "I have a knack for identi-fying teachers who are totally student-focused." She added, somewhat surprisingly, "I never ask a teacher to deliver a les-son; I ask lots of questions *not* about lessons." But Patton went on to explain that getting great teachers is not about hiring the best—it's about developing them, much as Barth described the strategy at KIPP.

Patton's approach is also similar. It begins with support. Over the years Patton has asked teachers to work long hours without extra compensation and to achieve high standards. To make these demands, Patton said she always believed that she needed to go above and beyond—as highlighted in chapter 2—to support her teachers. For San Jose Charter Academy that has always meant "constant opportunities to learn." It's meant regular training "beginning with the 'why' training is needed, then proceeding to the 'how' after teachers are bought in." It has also meant highly effective support personnel such as reading and math specialists, "not the irrelevant staff like in most schools." Patton is a huge believer in creating the conditions in which teachers could not imagine teaching anywhere else or being any more successful.

She is also no-nonsense when it comes to getting results for students. Each year she holds one-on-one "data conversations" with each teacher, offering her evaluation of what each teacher has accomplished and her expectations for the coming year. The focus is achievement data, from state tests to formative assessments. The data needle better be moving. Patton seldom asks a teacher to leave for poor performance. This is much different from the school's opening year, when "I dropped about a fourth of them." Very few exit voluntarily. The school is now a success. It has a great teacher in every classroom.

DISTRUSTING THE PRINCIPALS

If principals are going to fill their schools with highly effective teachers, they must have a certain set of skills. They must know great teaching. They must create constant opportunities for teachers to learn from experience and from one another. They must create positive cultures in which great teachers, regardless of the challenges of the students, want to stay. They must hold adults accountable, as Barth explained.

None of these skills is easy to develop. If they were, KIPP would not spend several years working to develop them in all of its principals. Knowing great teaching almost demands having been a great teacher oneself. Highly effective teachers are scarce. Great teachers may work wonders in their classrooms, but this does not mean that they will know how to share their talents or create a school-wide environment of excellence if they move into a leadership post. Holding adults accountable is a tough skill generally, one that many managers in fields beyond education struggle to do well.

But public education faces a much tougher problem than just developing challenging skills in its principals. Public education is fundamentally not set up to attract and retain the kind of talent necessary to become top principals. This is the nub of the problem.

Public education is really not designed for principals to be leaders. Principals are responsible for delivering education consistent with district, state, and federal policy. Higher authorities generally provide the principal with the curriculum, the instructional methods, and the ongoing assessments the school is expected to use. External policies prescribe how students with special needs, gifts, or language requirements are to be served. Great principals are supposed to inspire their schools with mission and vision. But the substance of these fundamentals is already established by others.

Crucially, principals are generally not given authority over their teachers. School districts almost universally screen potential teachers before principals get to consider them for employment. Tenure rules, in states with and without collective bargaining, constrain—indeed, virtually prohibit—principals from removing tenured teachers from their schools, notwith-standing ample evidence that teacher performance tends to decline after ten years on the job. Principals cannot reward a teacher financially for a job well done; compensation is set by the district and tied, almost without exception, to experience and degrees. In some school systems principals do not have final say over who teaches in their schools. Seniority rules can bump junior teachers, no matter how effective, and saddle a school with a more senior teacher, potentially less effective.

Prospective principals know the rules under which they will be required to lead. Aspirants driven by the desire to create a great school are likely to be turned off by the limitations that public school systems routinely impose upon their principals. They want an opportunity to build a zealous team of superior educators, craft a program of curriculum and instruction that the team can deliver, help the team members coalesce around a shared mission and vision, and take responsibility for results. Faced with the constraints of today's public school systems, potential go-getters may look outside of traditional systems for work in charter schools, such as KIPP. Or they may take a prin-cipal's post in a constrained school system and try to succeed by working around the rules. Or they may find the whole business too frustrating and instead choose to remain an effective teacher.

Not every prospective principal will feel this way, however. Some will aspire to succeed by the rules of traditional public school systems. They will gladly take on the role of principal as defined by the system. They will do their best to manage suc-cessfully by the rules. They will tend to the buses, buildings, bells, budgets, and behavior. If their schools run smoothly and achieve respectably, they may be offered promotions to higher posts in the school district, if that is what they desire. They will prove themselves as managers, if not as leaders.

Twenty years ago, Terry Moe and I conducted a comprehensive analysis of the attributes of effective schools, using test scores and surveys from over 10,000 students and from more than 10,000 teachers and their principals in a national sample of 400 schools.[26] We found that schools making top quartile achievement gains had stronger principals than schools making bottom quartile gains. Strong principals were regarded by teachers as having clearer goals. They held teaching in higher esteem. They became principals because they wanted to get control over their schools' educational programs and teams. Principals in low-achieving schools were more likely to have chosen the role to advance their careers or, to be blunt, because they preferred administration to teaching. The data, collected as part of a large-scale federal longitudinal analysis of high schools, confirmed what has now become commonplace in research and reform: successful principals are about teaching and leadership.

Our research discovered something much more striking. When we asked where the strong and weak principals were found, we learned that they worked in very different environments. The principals in low-achieving schools worked under conditions of high constraint over their discretion to control personnel and policy in their schools. These principals were severely limited in their ability to hire, transfer, and dismiss teachers. They faced seniority rules that were much more likely to force them to hire a demonstrably inferior candidate over a superior one. They also had much less say over curriculum and instruction. Less successful principals were hemmed in by superintendents, school boards, and teachers' unions. On average, the weak principals were 30 percent more likely than the strong principals to face above-average constraints.

The lesson in this is that school systems cannot expect to attract and retain principals who exert strong leadership unless they give them ample berth to lead. School systems have to provide their principals with meaningful autonomy if they want them to do what great principals do. Leading lights like McKinsey, Marzano, and countless other leadership authorities can exhort principals to be stronger instructional leaders. They can call for intensive training to lift principals above their mundane managerial responsibilities. But until public school systems change the rules under which they ask principals to operate—rules that often tie one arm behind their backs—all the leadership advice in the world is not going to produce stronger principals.

A Final Page from KIPP

When Terry Moe and I advocated greater autonomy for schools and principals in the early 1990s, the idea was relatively novel. In the years since, the recommendation has become routine. Impressive new organizations have emerged to help develop education leaders who can be entrusted with autonomy. The various leadership programs of the Eli Broad Foundation and New Leaders for New Schools have trained hundreds of principals and higher-level administrators in the new mold. Yet, school systems have not moved systematically to grant principals substantial autonomy. Teachers are still very much controlled and protected by personnel rules detailed in collective bargaining agreements and civil service policies. Education programs have become, if anything, more standardized as school systems aim to meet state achievement standards.

There is some danger, moreover, that principals are on the verge of even further constraints in promoting teacher effectiveness. Technology now permits the estimation of teacher value-added scores for all teachers who instruct tested subjects and grades. Formal evaluation rubrics, as discussed above, are making it possible for districts to obtain qualitative measures of teacher effectiveness, to complement quantitative value-added measures. The Obama administration has been encouraging the use of both measures in teacher evaluations to promote teacher quality. These metrics are potentially of great value: knowing with certainty who is helping students and who is not can facilitate more targeted teacher training and more appropriate teacher retention or de-selection decisions.

But there is real danger that these metrics will be used according to strict rules that tie the hands of principals and make it more difficult for them to develop strong teachers or build effective teams. In pitched battles over how teachers are to be evaluated, teacher's unions are pressing to have the new quantitative and qualitative measures of teacher performance translated automatically into ratings over which principals will have little or no control. Principals are resisting, and understandably so.[27] It is not hard to imagine a computer some day soon generating annual performance scores for all teachers—and the consequences associated with them, including raises, bonuses, tenure, retention, and promotion. Principals could find it difficult to exercise judgment about how teachers will be supported or deployed, retained or replaced. They could find it difficult to weigh qualitative factors such as fit and teamwork in building an effective staff. It is not difficult to imagine the further formalization of teacher evaluation making the job of principal even less attractive to potentially strong leaders.

Data are important, to be sure. Strong leaders will want to know the facts about their staffs and their schools. But strong leaders will also want to be trusted to use the data as they see fit to improve teachers and build a better school. Will school systems give principals this autonomy? If they do, how will they ensure that principals use it well?

Ironically, KIPP has struggled with this question for as long as it has been trying to get to scale. KIPP is not a public school system, at least not in the ordinary sense of the word. It is not subject to the political process in which various interest groups try to impose their views of school reform—and require principals to execute the plans. KIPP is free to provide principals whatever autonomy KIPP thinks best, without political pressure to do otherwise. At the same time, the KIPP Foundation wants to ensure quality schools and protect KIPP's reputation for extraordinary performance. Barth explained that KIPP was very conscious of the danger of creating a national bureaucracy. KIPP also knows that it has to cultivate the strongest education leadership possible, in its principals.

KIPP's answer has been twofold. First, KIPP created its intensive leadership development program that prepares every KIPP leader from grade level teacher chair to founding new school principal. KIPP controls leadership preparation, with its characteristic focus on great teaching. Second, KIPP created an accountability system that allows KIPP to give its principals substantial autonomy. KIPP does not specify curriculum or instruction or assessment in its schools. It leaves the program to the principal and school staff. KIPP does not constrain the hiring or development or management of the school staff. That is entirely in the hands of the principal. It's the principal's team and the principal's education program—the heart of what any strong principal wants to control.

The principal is accountable for working according to the five pillars of all KIPP schools. Then there is an accountability system, with teeth. All principals are evaluated annually by regional directors using the Leadership Competency Framework. This is important but hardly path-breaking. Far more important is KIPP's Healthy Schools dashboard. KIPP holds principals strictly accountable for six indicators: 1) Is the school serving the students KIPP wants? 2) Are the students staying? 3) Are the students making annual academic progress toward on-time entrance to college? 4) Are students graduating from college and pursuing education beyond? 5) Is the school sustainable for KIPP, as gauged by staff satisfaction and turnover? 6) Is the school sustainable financially?

Four of the indicators are about students while only two are about the school—reflections of KIPP's focus on achievement. The student indicators are far more ambitious than federal policy. No mention is made of Adequate Yearly Progress (AYP), the term of art under No Child Left Behind. KIPP's mission is college for all students, and all four indicators reflect that lofty goal. If KIPP schools hit these goals, AYP takes care of itself. KIPP makes sure that principals have to reach these goals by taking a long-term view of the staff and the school. Schools that post fast achievement gains but burn out staff in the process are not acceptable. Nor are schools that fail to add enrollment and wean themselves from excessive philanthropy.

KIPP has very rarely had to remove principals or pull schools' licenses for failing to perform against these six indicators. But KIPP has done so when necessary. More positively, KIPP's regional directors keep regular tabs on measures of the six indicators and work with principals throughout the school year to help them stay on track. The system has simplicity as a virtue. It is easy to know what counts for progress.

Public school systems do not have the luxury of providing principals autonomy and accountability in such a straightforward mix. KIPP is a system of charter schools relatively free from the political pressures that tend to impose reforms on traditional public schools and their principals. Like San Jose Charter, KIPP has been free to decide what is most important for student success and to build accordingly. Charter schools like these have decided quite explicitly that top teachers are the most important determinant of student achievement. They have further decided that principals are the best judge of talent and source of its development. Their principals have the autonomy to build effective teams. KIPP schools provide their leaders with unparalleled training to do so. Principals are then held strictly to account for teacher success.

KIPP and other charter schools that focus relentlessly on teacher and principal quality did not have to adopt these emphases. They did not have to provide autonomy and accountability as they have. No legislature or board of education mandated that they operate as they do. They also did not arrive where they are today following any grand plan. They achieved success over time learning from experience—and doing whatever was necessary to help students achieve. They chose leadership and teacher quality because they work.

Public schools cannot just choose to do what works. But public policymakers could make the teacher quality problem much simpler if they considered how public school principals could be encouraged, rewarded, and held accountable for the success of their teachers. There is no better time than the present to do so. The most common age bracket for public school principals is now over 55 years old—ten years higher than only a decade ago.[28] Public schools will need tens of thousands of new principals between now and 2020. If those principals are great teachers themselves, trained, empowered, and held to account for building effective teaching teams and raising student achievement, the teacher quality problem will be a long way toward being solved.

CHAPTER 5

Getting the Best

The most striking thing about the teacher quality problem is that we know how to do better—but refuse to do it. It is pretty obvious that high academic standards for students call for high academic standards for teachers. But schools routinely hire teachers with achievement below national averages. The shortcomings of America's 1,400 teacher education programs have been well documented for many years. But schools continue hiring new teachers from all of them. Instructional leadership has been the mantra for successful principals for as long as disappointing achievement has been an issue in America's schools. Yet school systems routinely appoint principals without regard to their success as teachers. Technology surrounds schools and offers potential solutions to students and teachers. But it is not much utilized.

Some of this behavior might be chalked up to ignorance. Research has only made crystal clear in the last decade the criticality of effective teachers. But much of the behavior of public schools and school systems is simply irrational—if their goal is to improve student achievement. Why else promote principals with no record of success in the classroom, or employ teachers with low aptitude, prepared in weak institutions? It does not really require mountains of research to know that these are likely to be bad decisions. Appreciating why public education makes bad decisions, especially about people, is crucial to reducing bad decisions in the future.

That begins with understanding that public schools are not irrational. They just are not set up to pursue single-mindedly student achievement as their goal. Yes, public schools are accountable for student progress. But they are also accountable for precisely how they help students achieve. They are accountable for following rules that prescribe how students will be educated. When it comes to people this means hiring teachers and principals who have been certified and licensed according to long-established rules and regulations that happen to favor 1,400 traditional schools of education. It means evaluating people with tools mandated in civil service legislation or collective bargaining agreements. It means granting tenure after several satisfactory years in the classroom. It means paying teachers for experience and advanced degrees, no matter how much research says the latter does not benefit achievement.

The rules that prescribe how schools are to pursue student achievement are products of the political process. They are legacies of political battles fought over generations, some during times when student achievement was not such a large issue. But whether achievement was a priority or not, other priorities were always present—particularly the welfare of the schools, colleges, and universities doing the educating and of the educators working in them. It requires no conspiracy theory or any animus toward the unions or associations that represent these interests to appreciate the way rules get made. It is a legitimate and predictable element of democratic politics that stakeholders with the most intense interest in an issue will wield the most influence, or at least hold considerable sway.

Politics has been particularly effective in blocking those poli-cies that are most threatening to employment in the system, including the public schools and the colleges and universities that support them.[1] Public education has been unable to adopt policies that hold teachers accountable for student achieve-ment, give principals real responsibility and accountability for teacher quality, or use technology to benefit students if jobs are threatened in the process. Public education has been unable systematically to attract the highest potential candidates into public education or reward strong performance. The preceding chapters reviewed the evidence, quantitative and qualitative, for these and related measures. It is increasingly clear what needs to be done if America really wants the best teachers in the world. The challenge is getting beyond the politics.

Policymakers can meet this challenge. They need to think about more than proven practices. They need to consider the *incentives* in public education that often discourage educators from doing what is best. They need to look for solutions that can insulate proven practices from political compromise. Teacher quality cannot be mandated. It needs to be in the inter-est of public educators to make it their highest priority. Follow-ing are descriptions of the most promising strategies for raising teacher quality—and for depoliticizing proven practice.

One: Put Principals in Charge of Teacher Quality

The surest route to a high-achieving school is a highly effective teacher in every classroom. This outcome cannot be mandated. Teacher effectiveness cannot be predicted from a resume at hir-ing. We know that candidates with higher aptitude or majors in certain subjects are more likely to succeed than the alterna-tives. But most of the effectiveness that teachers ultimately demonstrate develops on the job, and can be observed only after hiring. Heightened job qualifications, such as Praxis scores or GPAs, will not guarantee teacher quality.

Once on the job, teacher quality can now be gauged with value-added assessments and formal qualitative evaluations. These tools can be very helpful in raising teacher quality. But like more demanding job qualifications, they cannot ensure a highly effective teacher in every classroom. Whether teachers become highly effective depends on how well they learn from experience. That depends on the opportunities that they have to learn from highly successful colleagues, coaches—and their principals. If teachers become successful, they have to remain in their schools, if the schools are to benefit from their improvement.

School districts have attempted to formalize these processes. They have spent untold sums on teacher induction programs and ongoing professional development. They have provided incentives for teachers to continue teaching in challenging schools. But there is little evidence that these measures have worked. They do not really address what most affects teachers, and that is the daily experience in their schools.

Principals have most control over this experience—and they should. There is statistically significant evidence that principals have a substantial effect on student achievement. There is every reason to believe that this effect is exerted through the principal's influence over teachers. If principals are able, they look to hire teachers, whether new or experienced, who will be good fits with the team they are building and have the potential to grow and improve in that school's context. This requires judgment, of course. Good principals do not throw up their hands at the challenge of making good hires from resumes, and select new teachers at random. In fact, in the interest of team-building, principals will sometimes involve teacher leaders in making the final selections.

Principals establish the routines and schedules that support teachers in their growth. Such things as team meetings, mentoring relationships, peer observations, and the principal's informal supervision and coaching are largely at the principal's discretion. Effective principals judge which teachers could use more support and which teachers might be best to provide it. In the end, effective principals decide which teachers may not have the ability to become top performers and find ways to remove them from their schools. They also find ways to keep the effective and promising ones in place.

Unfortunately, there are no ways to mandate effective principal behavior. This is not a matter of required time observing classrooms or of rules for shared decision-making—to cite popular prescriptions. Effective leadership cannot be reduced to a formula. It must focus on teachers, to be sure. But there is no one best way for it to be carried out. There is evidence that effective principals have been successful teachers themselves, are instructional experts, and care more about leading the school to academic success than about anything else. But these tendencies do not reduce neatly to job requirements for the principal. School systems can look for these attributes in principal candidates—as KIPP does in prospective leaders. They do not offer a certain formula for success.

Policymakers should recognize that principals are in the best position of anyone in a school system to judge, cultivate, and retain talent. Policymakers should equip principals with tools and data, especially value-added assessments and formal observation tools. They should then leave in the hands of principals decisions about which teachers to hire, offer tenure to, promote, retain, and, if necessary, fire. It would be the principal's responsibility as well to organize the school to help teachers learn from their experience. It would be the principal's responsibility in the end to ensure a highly effective teacher is in every classroom.

In exchange for this autonomy, policymakers should hold principals strictly accountable for student achievement. Teachers need to know that their school leader is making decisions with achievement foremost in mind. They need to know that if the principal makes decisions that are not in the best interest of teacher quality, the principal will be held to account. Prospective principals need to know the new expectations as well. It will not be enough to run a quiet building. The principal will be expected to be *the* instructional leader. If instruction is not a prospect's passion and strong suit, application is probably not advised.

How accountability is to be enforced or rewarded is a detail left for policymakers to devise. Principals must be expected to deliver on state and federal academic performance requirements. Policymakers would need to set finite timetables for getting and staying on track. Principals who fail would face termination or demotion. Policymakers could also consider financial bonuses for ongoing success. The average principal's salary in the United States is $86,000.[2] If successful principals were given 50 percent bonuses, and every one of the nation's 90,000 principals succeeded in earning one, the total price tag would be $3.9 billion. That is 0.7 percent of the nation's total K–12 annual current expenditures. If the incentive produced anything close to the improvement in teacher quality it has the potential to produce, the price would be small indeed.

Many school systems will find it impossible to adopt all of this recommendation, or perhaps even any of it. Whatever the evidence or the logic, teachers and their representatives will resist this much authority being placed in the hands of principals. Historically, teachers have known too many principals who hadn't a clue about instruction or were cronies of the superintendent and could not be trusted to write fair or accurate evaluations of their work. In any case, teachers, like all employees, want to do all they can to control their evaluations, promotions, and compensation. Today, these things are all tied up in procedures and protections memorialized in legislation or collective bargaining agreements. As already discussed, teachers' unions are battling now to control the use of value-added assessments and formal observations in future teacher evaluation systems. They want to limit principal discretion as much as possible.

The United States is a federal system. Politics vary state by state. Some states and their constituent school districts will find it easier to increase principal responsibility. The federal government could encourage states to experiment with enhanced principal authority, much as the Obama administration has provided incentives for value-added assessments.[3] If the role of the principal has the predicted potential to drive teacher quality, the evidence from the early adopters may promote movement among the resistors. At least one virtue of America's federal system of education is the opportunity for experimentation. This is an idea that warrants it.

Yet, only a Pollyanna would believe that public schools will empower principals readily. A few states and districts will have the political support to do so. Most will not. Accordingly, policymakers should consider another way to pursue the recommendation. As KIPP demonstrates, policymakers have a ready-made option in charter schools. Charter schools have the freedom to do whatever it takes to be successful, without the direct influence of politics. If a charter school's leaders believe that empowered principals are the key to success, they can empower them. KIPP did not choose to place all of its chips on principals because they were mandated by charter school law to do so. They made this bet because the instincts and experience of the founders led them to believe it was the right thing to do.

Not all charter schools exalt strong leadership—though successful networks like Achievement First and Uncommon Schools seem to do so. Many charter schools have failed academically, whether they empowered principals or not. The point is not that charter schools are roaring successes. It is that charter schools provide an opportunity for experimentation that is often not politically possible in traditional school systems. They have a powerful incentive to figure out how to succeed academically, whatever the means. Their funding depends on their ability to attract students. Families tend to care about academic success when making their choices.

Today, the nation has over 5,000 charter schools serving nearly 2 million students. The growth of charter schools since the first was authorized in 1990 has been rapid. But ten states still do not allow charter schools. Few states fund charter schools on a par with traditional public schools. States limit enrollments and, notwithstanding Obama administration efforts to the contrary, limit the number that can operate.[4] Policymakers would do well to reconsider the obstacles to charter schools.[5] Broadly speaking, there is evidence of their success and knowledge of how to make them better.[6] For present purposes, they offer an invaluable arena for experimentation. The case for strong principals would not be nearly as compelling today without the evidence that KIPP has provided. Policymakers should look to a vigorous charter school sector to try out ideas that traditional schools find politically intractable.

Once proven in charter schools, new ideas will be easier for traditional schools to adopt. Traditional schools will also face competition from charter schools and from traditional public schools that are able to embrace what works despite the politics.

Experimentation and imitation will drive all schools forward—
if charter schools are allowed to compete. Asking principals to
lead the development of teacher quality is an idea that warrants
this support.

What about the training and licensure of principals? The
answer to that is probably obvious by now. There is no evidence
that traditional principal training in schools of education or
principal licensure has any effect on principal performance.
KIPP obviously does not require traditional preparation for its
principals—unless the state in which it is operating does. We
also do not know enough to design a training program that is
likely to work, and could therefore fairly be required. The most
compelling evidence, as reviewed in chapter 4, is that the best
preparation for school leadership is success in the classroom.
Interestingly, many high-achieving nations do not require specific training or certification for principals; the only requirement is experience as a teacher.[7] That is why principals abroad
are often called "head teachers."

Policymakers would do well to abandon the regulatory approach to principal quality as they should for teacher quality.
Policymakers should instead encourage experimentation in
methods of selecting, training, supervising, and rewarding principals. Policymakers should encourage innovation in leadership
development, as the Obama administration has done through i3
grants to KIPP and others for this purpose. In addition to encouraging autonomy for school principals by creating competitive
charter school sectors, policymakers should create incentives for
school districts to provide their principals with more authority over the teachers in their schools—and, of course, more
accountability for academic outcomes. That, after all, is what
great leaders want in any successful enterprise. It is also what
great principals have always delivered upon.

Two: Do Away with Teacher Licensure and Bring Transparency to Teacher Training

Notwithstanding mountains of research, the best ways to develop highly effective teachers have simply not been established. Most of what research has taught us is negative. Traditional teacher preparation and certification do not yield better teachers than alternative preparation programs that require much less time. Master's degrees do not raise teacher effectiveness. For generations, public schools have equated university-based teacher preparation and degrees with teacher quality. This is acting against the evidence.

Yet, there are more than shreds of evidence of teacher attributes that may predict success. Teachers from higher quality colleges and universities appear to be more successful in the classroom than teachers from lower quality institutions. These institutions also educate higher aptitude students and this may explain some of their apparent success. Cognitive ability is a predictor of teacher performance. But teaching that is consistent with new instructional frameworks is also associated with higher student achievement. These frameworks call for teaching that is intellectually sophisticated.

International experience suggests an intellectual paradigm as well. The highest achieving nations draw their teaching candidates from the upper ranks of high school graduates. They train them for four or five years in institutions of higher learning that are selective in admissions. Some countries place a premium on subject matter learning. Others emphasize pedagogy and developmental psychology. Either way, teacher preparation is an academically rigorous process.

Research also makes clear that teachers learn from experience. The most highly regarded preparation programs in the United States and abroad offer prospective teachers carefully scaffolded classroom experiences, introducing students step-by-step to the demands of teaching. Teacher candidates receive constant feedback on their classroom experiences. By the time candidates complete the program, they may have a year's worth of actual teaching experience. When they begin full-time teaching, they are more like second- or third-year teachers in effective schools, given the amount of well-guided experience they have had.

Vanderbilt's Peabody College exemplifies these traits in the United States. From the intellectual model of teaching to the balance of academic instruction and clinical experience, Peabody delivers what the most respected education schools in the world also deliver. It would be tempting to recommend that U.S. policymakers insist that all teachers be trained in institutions modeled after Peabody in rigor and approach. That is exactly what prominent studies of international practice have urged.[8]

But that would be a mistake. At the end of the day, the question still remains whether teachers from esteemed institutions are succeeding because of the preparation that they received or because of the native talent that they bring to the job. In this country, policymakers must take seriously the success of Teach for America, which has excelled with teachers offered a fraction of the usual pre-service preparation. TFA teachers, like top teachers internationally or teachers from institutions like Peabody, have received an outstanding academic education. But they have entered the school classroom with only five weeks of formal preparation. Teachers trained in the Peabody mode have had perhaps twenty times the training, in clinical experience and education course work. Rigorous measures of performance have not distinguished differences in their classroom effectiveness. They both seem to work very well.

So, what should policymakers do? Policymakers should endeavor first to determine what teacher preparation actually helps teachers raise student achievement. State data systems will soon make it possible for most, if not all, states to measure the effectiveness of all public school teachers who instruct subjects assessed by the state. Those same systems can be used to gauge the value added by the graduates of various teacher training programs. State data systems would merely need to include the name of the institution and the program of study from which each teacher received a degree or certificate. Tennessee has been doing this for several years, and now calculates several measures of program effectiveness, as highlighted in chapter 3. Louisiana and several other states have similar systems under development.[9]

Measurement systems could evaluate various preparation routes. They could compare institutions offering four-year baccalaureate programs. They could compare master's degree programs pursued after a non-education bachelor's degree, to prepare for a first teaching job. They could compare master's programs taken after a teacher is already working in the classroom. Measurement systems could also measure programs that provide alternate routes to the classroom. Teach for America is but one example. The New Teacher Project is another. Measurement could also be trained on district-sponsored induction programs and ongoing professional development programs provided externally or internally.

Research has generally found little to recommend training or preparation programs. But that may be because research focuses on the average effects of different types of training. For example, do master's degrees, as a general category of training, boost achievement? The answer to that question has been generally negative. But that does not mean that some master's programs are not highly effective—or that others are counterproductive. What the Tennessee data show are a couple of programs being very effective, namely Peabody and TFA. The data also flag several colleges and universities producing teachers with inferior performance. Most programs occupy middle ground. Policymakers should be less concerned with what types of training work and more concerned with which specific institutions or providers work.

New data systems can also be used to help answer the question: is a teacher preparation program effective, given the quality of student it admits? Are the Tennessee programs that graduate unusually high numbers of bottom quartile teachers doing so because their students are low aptitude or because the training program is lacking? Similarly, is Peabody turning out top quartile teachers in higher numbers because of the unusually high aptitude of its undergraduates, or because of the quality of its program? To be clear, schools looking to hire high-potential teachers should care most about the caliber of a program's graduates, and not whether the institution or the student is more responsible for the outcome. But training programs could use the information for improvement. States and accreditation agencies could use the information for evaluating teacher preparation programs, if they desired.

Data systems might finally be expanded to include measures of teacher effectiveness obtained from validated formal observational tools. States are now rapidly adopting these, and research is confirming their reliability and validity. They add significantly to the ability of value-added measures to predict student achievement. With value-added scores they provide a more well-rounded measure of teacher effectiveness. Which preparation programs are responsible for teachers with high qualitative *and* quantitative effectiveness scores? That's even more valuable information. Qualitative measures have an additional virtue. They can be obtained for all teachers, and not for only those who teach subjects tested by the states. With qualitative measures, states can look at preparation programs for primary teachers or teachers of the arts. The system could be comprehensive.

Policymakers should build these data systems and estimate the effectiveness of each program's participants. They should then take one further critical step. They should make the information public. Schools and school systems need to know the track records of the programs from which they are selecting new teachers. They need to know the performance of teachers who attend programs offering advanced degrees. They need to know how teachers perform who have participated in various professional development programs. Schools and school systems are free to use the information any way they wish. But if they are accountable for student achievement, they will surely tend to favor programs with strong records of helping teachers succeed. Prospective students will be swayed by this information as well. Why attend a school of education whose graduates have not fared well as teachers, especially knowing that the schools and districts doing the hiring know about the short-coming, too?

Policymakers should summarize information on effectiveness in simple metrics. They might consider rating programs with an A–F letter grade. Value-added analyses can get quite technical. Policymakers should ensure that the evaluations are easy for participants and employers to understand. Scores should also be easily accessible. They should certainly be posted on state websites. States might also require all institutions providing training or candidates to public schools to post their effectiveness scores on their own websites.

The idea behind these reforms is to drive improvement in training through competition among training institutions, based on performance. The 1,400 colleges and universities that train teachers today already compete for students. But students have no real idea how well-prepared they will be to teach after graduation. Employers—schools and school districts—have no reliable idea about the quality of candidates that different institutions produce. If, in the future, participants and employers both knew the effectiveness of teacher preparation or professional development programs, successful programs would tend to grow or be imitated and unsuccessful programs would tend to improve or go out of business.

Information can be a powerful lever for change. Policymakers do not have to mandate new forms of training. They do not have to hold training programs accountable or consider closing down dubious institutions. All policymakers need to do is ensure that decision-makers in the marketplace for training are much better informed about what works. They will tend to choose effectiveness when they know where to find it. Now that data and technology make it possible to calculate what works, policymakers have ready access to the lever.

In recent years policymakers have gained experience using this lever to improve higher education more generally. With half of all undergraduates never completing a four-year degree, the cost of higher education outstripping inflation for decades, and students leaving college burdened with loan debt, policymakers have taken to shining a bright light on school track records. The Higher Education Act of 2008 mandated colleges and universities to report substantial performance data, now publicized on the federal Department of Education website. The Obama administration upped the ante in 2012 by proposing a more revealing "college scorecard," including job placement rates. It is not a great stretch for policymakers to publicize the effectiveness of teacher training institutions.

To be sure, information is not a panacea. Prospective teachers, like prospective college students in other fields, make many bad decisions today. They enroll in institutions with poor graduation rates—information that is already available. But students are only half of the marketplace, and success scores would add a major new data point to their decision-making. The other half of the market—employers—can be counted on to be more quality-conscious. If principals and schools are held more strictly to account for student achievement, and if they have discretion over who to hire, they will pay much greater attention to where teachers have been trained if they have easy access to measures of effectiveness. They will also look more carefully at how teachers receive ongoing external training, if measures of the effectiveness of that training are available. Better decisions by employers will improve the quality of options from which students have to choose, even if students are not astute choosers themselves.

To put faith in information to drive improvement in teacher training, policymakers must take one final initiative. They should end teacher licensure as we know it. Given the lack of firm knowledge of how best to prepare teachers for the classroom, state policymakers should lift all public school teaching requirements other than a bachelor's degree and a background check for public school teachers. Yes, that is right. It makes no sense to require specific forms of training or testing when there is no evidence that those requirements improve teaching. The federal government should also lift the "highly qualified teacher" provisions of the Elementary and Secondary Education Act that mandate certification. Schools and school systems should be free to decide what training they want to require. They may still prefer traditional four-year university-based programs. But they should be free to choose TFA-like programs without layering on alternative certification requirements, if they wish. Private schools, it should be noted, decide on their own what additional training they want to see in their teachers, without government mandate. Eliminating licensure is not a far-fetched idea.

In an open market for teacher training, programs like Peabody's that seem to be exemplary will be likely to receive high marks, thrive, and proliferate. Third-tier college-based programs will face wake-up calls and will have to improve to keep attracting students. More programs like TFA that emphasize smart, fresh graduates and intensive on-the-job coaching are likely to emerge. Programs for second-career professionals who want to bring their wisdom and expertise to the classroom are also likely to appear. As long as policymakers measure and publicize the effectiveness of these myriad programs and institutions, the quality of teacher preparation should improve.

With time, particular types of teacher preparation may appear to be superior. Policymakers may then be tempted to require such training of all teachers—and restore the type of certification and licensure we have known for generations. They should resist the temptation. Training should not be locked in place with the discovery that a particular approach is effective. Teaching is likely to continue to evolve, especially with the introduction of educational technology. Training programs should always have the incentive to innovate and improve, not to fall in line behind one tried-and-true approach that worked for a time. Colleges, universities, and other institutions that provide pre-service and in-service teacher training should forever be encouraged to improve their effectiveness. Policymakers should focus on measuring and publicizing what works.

Three: Use Technology to Make Teaching a More Selective, More Productive, and Better Compensated Profession

It makes no sense to insist that teachers alone help students reach high levels of achievement. In education, as in virtually every field of human endeavor, technology is offering more effective and efficient ways to proceed. Yet, our schools—public and private alike—rely almost completely on whole-group instruction by individual teachers to help students achieve. The model is inherently limited, due to the individual needs of students. One teacher cannot give every student optimally what he or she needs, regardless of how smart or well-prepared that teacher may be. Class sizes can be reduced—and have been substantially reduced already—to make the job more manageable. But class size reductions that might move the needle of achievement as far as the United States requires are prohibitively expensive. They're also unnecessary. Education need not be made more labor-intensive and less efficient to succeed. Education can make progress like every other industry, to the benefit of students and of teachers.

Technology offers proven answers already. As detailed in chapter 2, technology can be used with students at all ages to supplement instruction by teachers, providing differentiated remediation or acceleration. It can also be used to provide the core instruction for whole courses, supplemented by teachers online or face-to-face in limited ways. Technology can relieve the teacher of burdensome responsibility for communicating content—like a much more sophisticated textbook. It can provide students more opportunity for individually guided practice than a teacher ever could. Technology can provide fine-tuned assessments and diagnostics.

By relieving teachers of work they need not do and providing teachers with intelligence on what individual students need, technology can give teachers more time and ability to handle higher-level instructional challenges. Teachers can focus more on helping students with creative work like research, analysis, problem-solving, and writing, or on tutoring specific needs. Scores of schools around the United States are now demonstrating the benefit of blending teachers and technology. Evidence is growing that students can learn well with technology and that teachers can be more effective with more focused and vital roles.

Schools have been slow, however, to adopt technology, especially for core instruction. Public schools are government institutions, guided by the political process and largely shielded from competitive pressures—save for the small charter school sector. Schools can therefore tolerate the inertia that slows change in any large organization: who wants to change if they do not have to? But schools have been able to apply another much stronger brake. The status quo is protected by the political process itself when change threatens employment in the system. Employees have a political upper hand. Policymakers who may want to see more technology in the schools cannot easily mandate it. If changing the mix of teachers and technology costs jobs, the opposition to technology can be fierce.

But policymakers should not want to *mandate* technology. This is key. No one knows what the right mix of technology and teachers is for different subjects, grade levels, and students. Even if the mix were known today, it would change tomorrow, with advances in technology. Progress will not come in the form of required uses of technology—like a mandatory online course for graduation. The answer comes in freeing up decision-making about teachers and technology so that there is incentive and opportunity for schools to find the right mixture to maximize student success. Currently, policy places too many barriers in the way of technology and provides schools too few incentives to experiment with it.

Policymakers should be looking at ways to allow technological solutions to compete with traditional instruction and thereby encourage schools to reconsider the mix of technology and teachers they are employing. Policymakers could adopt these measures without forcing anyone to change what they are doing. The right measures would provide opportunity and incentives. How schools reacted to them would be for schools to decide. In the end, what is most effective and efficient should prevail.

The essential measures are the following:

1. States should allow online charter schools to operate statewide, providing students and families with access to full-time technology-based education if they like. Online charter schools would also provide incentive for traditional schools to offer online options or risk losing students to online charters.

2. States should guarantee students access to part-time online learning, for example, for individual courses, whether the student's home school offers such courses or not. Courses might be offered by online charter schools, state virtual schools, or other state authorized providers. Students would then be guaranteed online instruction, part-time, if they wanted it, and their home schools would have incentives to provide technology-based instruction itself.

3. States should provide equal per-pupil funding for traditional and online instruction, whether full-time or part-time, the latter funded on a pro-rata basis. Online providers should compete with one another and with traditional brick-and-mortar schools to provide the best full-time or part-time education possible, for a common price.

There are additional details to which policymakers would need to attend, such as oversight and accountability.[10] But various states have been developing options. And research continues to identify best practices. The most important thing for policymakers is to create opportunities for students and their families to choose technology-based education full-time or part-time and for traditional public schools to have incentives to adopt technology themselves. This last point is vital.

Almost no one believes that the best education for most students is full-time online learning. Students need face-to-face social interaction for their personal development and for their education. Most families need their children to be supervised in schooling while parents or caregivers work. The future of education technology is therefore most likely to be dominated by blended institutions in which students receive some instruction via technology and some face-to-face. Technology will do what it does best. Teachers will provide instruction where they can add the most value. The mix may differ by student, grade level, and subject. Experimentation will yield different mixes, and they will evolve over time with advances in technology. If policymakers get the opportunities and incentives right, schools will make choices in the best interest of students, with the dollars they are given.

Technological innovation, driven by a competitive market, will almost certainly result in students learning more through technology and less through teachers. If students are learning more as a result, this is clearly a good thing. Fairly modest increases in student time with technology can reduce demand for teachers materially. The model in chapter 2, a lower-bound estimate, assumed one hour of technology per day for students in kindergarten through fifth grade, two hours for grades six through eight, and three hours for grades nine through twelve. The need for teachers in this model dropped from 3.2 million nationally to about 2.6 million. This reduction could go a long way toward solving the teacher quality problem. It means 600,000 fewer high-quality teachers need to be found.

More important, the reduced demand for teachers provides a dividend that could be used to pay deserving teachers more.

The teaching profession in the United States has lost access to high-potential female teachers over the last forty years as salaries for teachers have fallen compared to other professions and as employment opportunities for bright women have increased. U.S. schools pay teachers less, as a share of GDP, than at least a dozen higher achieving nations—this despite the United States being a high spender on education, gauged by GDP, overall. U.S. education dollars do not go to individual teachers. If this country is going to attract and retain higher caliber male and female teachers, it must reward successful teachers more.

The United States could raise taxes to pay for those rewards. But international comparisons do not justify that. The country could reduce its spending on school and district support staff—the main differentiator of U.S. spending patterns from those around the world. But that is a different matter altogether, with its own political challenges. Or the United States could allow technological innovation to take its course and identify efficiencies. It is likely that that path would help students as well as teachers become more successful. And it would yield a financial dividend.

Reduced demand for teachers could save close to $39 billion per year, as chapter 2 explained. That savings could be used to provide $29,000 annual bonuses for the top half of all public school teachers nationwide. It could also be used to reward, in the most dramatic way, the very best teachers. Top quartile teachers can make remarkable differences in student achievement. Several consecutive years with top quartile teachers can literally change the life of a disadvantaged, low-performing student. What if the technology dividend were used to reward only the top quartile of teachers? Their bonuses would be $58,000. That would more than double the income of top teachers to $112,000 per year. The best teachers in the world would be the best-paid teachers in the world.

That would be the clearest statement that the United States really does want the best.

It's Fundamental

The United States needs substantially stronger teachers if it is to have any hope of equaling or surpassing the achievement of the top-performing nations in the world. Teachers who themselves achieve far below the expected achievement of their students simply will not do. Nor will teachers trained and certified in sub-par institutions. Nor will teachers on the job who consistently fall into the bottom quartile of performance. Nor will principals who do not know instruction. These conditions not only suppress the nation's achievement by allowing weak teachers to teach. They hold the country back by discouraging strong teachers from joining or remaining in the profession.

The measures recommended here to raise teacher quality are intended fundamentally to change that profession. Great teachers do not want what manicurists want—a license to practice from the state. They want much more. They want training that is demanding, not perfunctory. They want to be judged and recognized for their performance, not treated like interchangeable parts. They want to work with leaders whom they respect for their knowledge of the craft. They embrace innovation that might enable them to help more students succeed. They have alternatives in life and want a profession that rewards them for the vital work that education surely is. They expect to be held accountable.

That is not the profession that public education provides teachers today. And, even the most promising reform measures, such as strengthening teacher evaluations, will not really change the profession—certainly not enough to alter materially the caliber of educators who join and remain. The strategy recommended here is different. It is meant to change the incentives and opportunities for educators themselves to re-create their profession. The strategy does not look to policymakers to strengthen the profession. It looks to policymakers to give educators the freedom and reason to do so. It looks to policymakers to give educators the information to make good decisions. The decision-making authority rests with the educators—with the professionals.

So, policymakers are not asked to tell educators who they can and cannot hire. Policymakers are instead asked to provide educators with information about who has been well-trained and who has not. Similarly, educators are not to be told who to retain or promote or let go. Policymakers will provide value-added estimates of teacher effectiveness and rigorous qualitative assessments of instruction, but the judgments are in the hands of the professionals. Much the same with technology: policymakers should not tell schools how to use technology, how to reap savings, or how to use the savings to improve teacher compensation. Policymakers should ensure that schools have powerful incentives to experiment and adopt.

In exchange for the freedom, schools and, especially, school leaders must be held strictly to account for student progress. That is the bargain that professionals should want—autonomy to control their work fully, to be compensated for it fairly, and to accept responsibility for its results. This is a very different arrangement than the one that has long governed education— and that now impedes the improvement of teacher quality. Policymakers need to take a fundamentally different approach. Teacher quality cannot be prescribed.

Given strong incentives to perform and the information to do so, the American educational system will improve teacher training. It will select, develop, and retain teachers who perform best for students. It will incorporate technology to boost productivity and teacher compensation. And it will promote and reward school leaders who make decisions in the best interests of students and teachers. This book has tried through careful review of the scientific evidence and illustrations of the ideas at work to show what is possible. There is no material reason why the United States cannot have the best teachers in the world. More than anything, it requires a willingness to let go of an approach, rooted in prescription and regulation, which has outlived its usefulness. This will not be easy politically. But nothing fundamental ever is. In the final analysis, if the nation wants an educational profession that is home to the best and the brightest, it will need to trust the profession and hold the profession strictly accountable for doing the right things.

Notes

Chapter 1

1. http://grad-schools.usnews.rankingsandreviews.com/best-graduate
-schools/top-education-schools.

2. Dartmouth College, a top twenty "national university," does not have a school of education, but does offer undergraduate teacher preparation for elementary and secondary education. Northwestern and Rice universities offer secondary teacher preparation, but no elementary teacher preparation for undergraduates.

3. This is based on data provided to the author by Peabody College of Education and Human Development (hereafter Peabody College) in December 2011.

4. See, for example, Michael Barber and Mona Mourshed, *How the World's Best Performing School Systems Come Out on Top*, McKinsey & Company, 2007; Byron Auguste, Paul Kihn, and Matt Miller, *Closing the Talent Gap: Attracting and Retaining Top-Third Graduates to a Career in Teaching*, McKinsey & Company, September 2010; and Marc S. Tucker, *Standing on the Shoulders of Giants: An American Agenda for Education Reform* (Washington, DC: National Center on Education and the Economy, May 24, 2011).

5. Rita Kramer, *Ed School Follies: The Miseducation of America's Teachers* (New York: Free Press, 1991); David F. Labaree, *The Trouble with Ed Schools* (New Haven, CT: Yale University Press, 2006).

6. Arthur Levine, *Educating School Teachers* (Washington, DC: The Education Schools Project, September 2006).

7. Julie Greenberg, Laura Pomerance, and Kate Walsh, *Student Teaching in the United States* (Washington, DC: National Council on Teacher Quality, July 2011).

8. Thomas J. Kane, Jonah E. Rockoff, and Douglas O. Staiger, "What Does Teacher Certification Tell Us About Teacher Effectiveness? Evidence From New York City," *Economics of Education Review*, vol. 27, no. 6 (December 2008), pp. 615–31; Dan Goldhaber, "Licensure: Exploring the Value of this Gateway to the Teacher Workforce," in *Handbook of the Economics of Education, vol. 3*, eds. Eric A. Hanushek, Stephen Machin, and Ludger Woessmann (Amsterdam: New Holland, forthcoming), pp. 315–39.

9. Auguste, Kihn, and Miller, *Closing the Talent Gap*, p. 14.

10. See, for example, Paul T. Decker, Daniel P. Mayer, and Steven Glazerman, *The Effects of Teach for America on Students: Findings from a National Evaluation* (Princeton, NJ: Mathematica Policy Research, June 9, 2004).

11. The evidence on this point is overwhelming. For a review of the evidence and estimates of its value to students and nations, see Eric A. Hanushek, "The Economic Value of Higher Teacher Quality," *Economics of Education Review*, vol. 30, no. 3 (June 2011), pp. 466–79. Recent evidence suggests that some curriculum programs may have comparable effects to teachers, but curriculum as a whole is not supported by such evidence. See Matthew M. Chingos and Grover J. "Russ" Whitehurst, *Choosing Blindly: Instructional Materials, Teacher Effectiveness, and the Common Core* (Washington, DC: The Brookings Institution, April 12, 2012).

12. In addition to Hanushek's "Economic Value," see Bryan C. Hassel and Emily Ayscue Hassel, *Opportunity at the Top: How America's Best Teachers Could Close the Gaps, Raise the Bar, and Keep Our Nation Great* (Chapel Hill, NC: Public Impact, 2010).

13. Barber and Mourshed, *World's Best Performing School Systems*, p. 16.

14. *Times Higher Education*, World University Rankings, http://www .timeshighereducation.co.uk/world-university-rankings.

15. The U.S. Department of Education conducted a study of mathematics achievement in which student level test scores in the National Education Longitudinal Study of 1988 (NELS:88) were "equated" with scores in the National Assessment of Educational Progress (NAEP). Rich NELS:88 longitudinal data were then used to analyze NAEP performance levels. NAEP performance levels are *below basic, basic, proficient,* and *advanced.*

The study found that among students with SAT math scores of 510–600, 61.2 percent scored *basic* and 37.7 percent scored *proficient* on NAEP. Among students with SAT math scores of 610–700, 15.4 percent scored *basic* and 73.5 percent scored *proficient* (and another 10.5 percent scored *advanced*). This suggests that attaining an NAEP *proficient* level requires a minimum of SAT 600. See Leslie A. Scott and Steven J. Ingels, *Interpreting 12th-Graders' NAEP-Scaled Mathematics Performance Using High School Predictors and Postsecondary Outcomes From the National Education Longitudinal Study of 1988 (NELS:88)* (NCES 2007–238), National Center for Education Statistics, Institute of Education Sciences, U.S. Department of Education, September 2007.

16. Drew H. Gitomer, *Teacher Quality in a Changing Policy Landscape: Improvements in the Teacher Pool* (Princeton, NJ: Educational Testing Service, September 2007).

17. The Educational Testing Service, "The Praxis Series: Passing Scores by State and Test" (Princeton, NJ: November 1, 2011). See Gitomer, *Teacher Quality*, for SAT scores of prospective teachers who pass or fail Praxis.

18. For an overview of international compensation variations, see Auguste, Kihn, and Miller, *Closing the Talent Gap*, pp. 12–15.

Chapter 2

1. U.S. Department of Education, *Digest of Education Statistics*, Institute of Education Sciences, National Center for Education Statistics, 2010, table 73.

2. Ibid., tables 68 and 73.

3. Ibid., table 73.

4. U.S. Department of Education, "2008 Long-Term Trend Top Stories," The Nation's Report Card, http://nationsreportcard.gov/ltt_2008.

5. Organization for Economic Co-operation and Development (OECD), *PISA 2009 Results: What Students Know and Can Do: Student Performance in Reading, Mathematics and Science (vol. I)*.

6. On class size reduction, see Alan B. Krueger, "Understanding the Magnitude and Effect of Class Size on Student Achievement," in *The Class Size Debate*, eds. Lawrence Mishel and Richard Rothstein (Washington, DC: Economic Policy Institute, 2002), pp. 7–35; and Grover J. "Russ" Whitehurst and Matthew M. Chingos, *Class Size: What Research Says and What It Means for State Policy* (Washington, DC: The Brookings Institution, May 11, 2011).

On master's degrees and experience effects, see Eric A. Hanushek and Steven G. Rivkin, "Teacher Quality," in *Handbook of the Economics of Education, vol. 2,* eds. Eric A. Hanushek and Finis Welch (Amsterdam: New Holland, 2006), pp. 1051–78.

7. The U.S. population has become more heterogeneous socio-economically over the last fifty years, making the task of teachers in heterogeneous communities more difficult. Some effects of class size, experience, and teacher education may be masked by the increasing challenge of the job. This has never been established in research, however.

8. For a range of perspectives, see Adam Gamoran, "Is Ability Grouping Equitable?" *Educational Leadership,* vol. 50, no. 2 (1992); Jeannie Oakes, *Keeping Track: How Schools Structure Inequality, 2nd ed.* (New Haven, CT: Yale University Press, 2005); and James A. Kulik and Chen-Lin C. Kulik, "Meta-analytic Findings on Grouping Programs," *Gifted Children Quarterly,* vol. 36, no. 2 (Spring 1992), pp. 73–77.

9. This section is based on an interview with Mike Kerr on November 17, 2011. Additional information was drawn from Mike Kerr, *KIPP: Empower Academy: A Blended Learning Model for Primary Grades,* Los Angeles: KIPP LA Schools, 2011, and *KIPP Empower Academy,* NewSchools Summit, May 2011.

10. In May 2012 Kim was named Educational Entrepreneur of the Year by the New Schools Venture Fund.

11. For more on Anthony Kim and Pennsylvania Cyber Charter School, see Terry M. Moe and John E. Chubb, *Liberating Learning: Technology, Politics, and the Future of American Education* (San Francisco: Jossey Bass, 2009), chap. 4.

12. For the latest on technology adoption in K–12 schools, see John Watson, Amy Murin, Lauren Vashaw, Butch Gemin, and Chris Rapp, *Keeping Pace with K–12 Online Learning: An Annual Review of Policy and Practice* (Durango, CO: Evergreen Education Group, 2011).

13. This section is based on an interview with Michelle Tubbs on December 21, 2011, documents subsequently provided by Tubbs, and information available on the school's website, http://www.laalliance.org/schools/atams.

14. This section is based on information available from the California Department of Education website, the San Jose Charter Academy website, and an interview with Principal Denise Patton on December 23, 2011. As background, the author visited San Jose Charter Academy several times from

1999–2009 while the school was part of the Edison Schools organization, and the author was Edison's chief education officer.

15. San Jose Charter Academy left the Edison network as a full member school in 2011, though it continues to purchase some technology and professional development services from the company.

16. The Dayton experiences, which launched in 2007, a year ahead of San Jose, are discussed in Moe and Chubb, *Liberating Learning*, chap. 4.

17. The "Lexile" is a widely-used unit of measurement that gauges the difficulty of reading material on a continuous scale covering material from kindergarten through high school. Most reading materials in U.S. schools today have a Lexile score reflecting their level of reading difficulty. Students' reading proficiency can also be measured with Lexile scores, reflecting the difficulty of material students are able to comprehend effectively.

18. Krueger, *Effect of Class Size*.

19. See, for example, Robert E. Slavin, Nancy A. Madden, and Robert J. Stevens, "Cooperative Learning Models for the 3 R's," *Educational Leadership*, vol. 47, no. 4 (December 1989), pp. 22–28; and Geoffrey D. Borman, Robert E. Slavin, Alan Cheung, Anne Chamberlain, Nancy A. Madden, and Bette Chambers, "Final Reading Outcomes of the National Randomized Field Trial of Success for All," *American Educational Research Journal,* vol. 44, no. 3 (September 2007), pp. 701–31.

20. Heather Staker, *The Rise of K–12 Blended Learning: Profiles of Emerging Models* (Mountain View, CA: Innosight Institute, May 2011).

21. On public school uses of technology, see Watson, et al., *Keeping Pace*; Anthony G. Picciano and Jeff Seaman, *K–12 Online Learning: A 2008 Follow-up of the Survey of U.S. School District Administrators* (Newburyport, MA: The Sloan Consortium, January 2009); and Matthew Wicks, *A National Primer on K–12 Online Learning, Version 2* (Vienna, VA: International Association for K–12 Online Learning, October 2010).

22. Clayton M. Christensen, Michael B. Horn, and Curtis W. Johnson, *Disrupting Class: How Disruptive Innovation Will Change the Way the World Learns* (New York: McGraw Hill, 2008).

23. Moe and Chubb, *Liberating Learning*, chap. 6.

24. For empirical evidence, see Terry M. Moe, *Special Interest: Teachers Unions and America's Public Schools* (Washington, DC: The Brookings Institution, 2011).

25. Gregg Vanourek, *An (Updated) Primer on Virtual Charter Schools: Mapping the Electronic Frontier* (Chicago: National Association of Charter School Authorizers, September 2011).

26. Brian D. Ray, *2.04 Million Homeschool Students in the United States in 2010* (Salem, OR: National Home Education Research Institute, January 2011).

27. Matt Richtel, "Teachers Resist High-Tech Push in Idaho Schools," *New York Times*, January 4, 2012.

28. Watson, *Keeping Pace*.

29. Barbara Means, Yukie Toyama, Robert Murphy, Marianna Bakia, and Karla Jones, *Evaluation of Evidence-Based Practices in Online Learning: A Meta-Analysis and Review of Online Learning Studies* (Washington, DC: U.S. Department of Education, revised September 2010).

30. Dan Goldhaber, "The Mystery of Good Teaching," *Education Next,* vol. 2, no. 2 (Spring 2002), pp. 50–55.

31. Hanushek and Rivkin, "Teacher Quality."

32. On the consequences of No Child Left Behind for state academic standards, see John E. Chubb, *Learning from No Child Left Behind: How and Why the Nation's Most Important But Controversial Education Law Should be Renewed* (Stanford, CA: Hoover Institution Press, 2009). On Common Core Standards, see http://www.corestandards.org.

33. Scott and Ingels, *Interpreting Mathematics Performance*.

34. SAT scores of new teachers have inched higher over the last decade as *No Child Left Behind* required teachers to pass Praxis I and II for certification. See Gitomer, *Teacher Quality*.

35. See especially Auguste, Kihn, and Miller, *Closing the Talent Gap*.

36. Sean P. Corcoran, "Human Capital Policy and the Quality of the Teacher Workforce," in *Creating a New Teaching Profession,* eds. Dan Goldhaber and Jane Hannaway (Washington, DC: The Urban Institute Press, 2009), chap. 3.

37. Marigee P. Bacolod, "Do Alternative Opportunities Matter? The Role of Female Labor Markets in the Decline of Teacher Quality," *Review of Economics and Statistics*, vol. 89, no. 4 (November 2007), pp. 737–51.

38. Corcoran, "Human Capital Policy," pp. 32–33.

39. For this and subsequent GDP spending percentages, see *Digest of Education Statistics*, 2010, table 426.

40. Ibid., table 429.

41. For salaries relative to GDP, see Dan Goldhaber, "Lessons from Abroad: Exploring Cross-Country Differences in Teacher Development Systems and What They Mean for U.S. Policy," in *Creating a New Teaching Profession*, chap. 5.

42. South Korea, for example, pays the top teacher salaries in the world and averages about thirty-five students per class. See Auguste, Kihn, and Miller, *Closing the Talent Gap*, pp. 13, 20–21.

43. Compensation of instructional staff represents only 61 percent of current annual education expenditures in U.S. public schools—a percentage that excludes all capital expenditures and indicates that one out of three school system employees is doing something other than classroom teaching.

44. For more on this model, see John E. Chubb, "More Productive Schools Through Online Learning," in *Stretching the School Dollar: How Schools and Districts Can Save Money While Serving Students Best*, eds. Frederick M. Hess and Eric Osberg (Cambridge, MA: Harvard Education Press, 2010), chap. 6.

45. *Digest of Education Statistics*, 2010, table 415.

46. Ibid., table 69.

47. John Marvel, Deanna M. Lyter, Pia Peltola, Gregory A. Strizek, and Beth A. Morton, *Teacher Attrition and Mobility: Results from the 2004–05 Teacher Follow-up Survey* (Washington, DC: Institute of Education Sciences, National Center for Education Statistics, U.S. Department of Education, 2007).

48. William J. Hussar and Tabitha M. Bailey, *Projections of Education Statistics to 2020* (Washington, DC: Institute of Education Sciences, National Center for Education Statistics, U.S. Department of Education, September 2011), figure 12.

49. *Digest of Education Statistics*, table 285.

50. Ibid.

51. The leading associations connected with online charter schools—the National Association of Charter School Authorizers and the International Association for K–12 Online Learning—put the savings from online charter schools at up to 15 percent. See Susan Patrick and Tom Vander Ark, *Viewpoint: Authorizing Online Learning*, National Association of Charter School Authorizers, August 2011. Slightly higher estimates of savings have recently been provided by the Parthenon Group: Tamara Butler Battaglino, Matt Haldeman, and Eleanor Laurans, "The Costs of Online Learning," in

Education Reform for the Digital Era, eds. Daniela R. Fairchild and Chester E. Finn Jr. (Washington, DC: Thomas B. Fordham Institute, January 2012).

52. *Digest of Education Statistics*, table 108.

53. Reducing the ratio of computers to students in high schools from 1:3 to 1:2 means providing one-sixth more computers. Even if fully loaded laptops were purchased for $1,000 each, the per-student incremental cost would be one-sixth of that, or $166. If that were amortized over three years—which is standard—the annual incremental high school computer cost is $55. Working off of a $1,000-per-computer price tag makes this estimate conservative.

54. *Digest of Education Statistics*, table 188.

55. Ibid.

56. *Digest of Education Statistics*, table 82.

57. On the use of compensation to improve teacher quality, see Peter Dolton and Oscar D. Marcenaro-Gutierrez, "If You Pay Peanuts, Do You Get Monkeys? A Cross-Country Analysis of Teacher Pay and Pupil Performance," *Economic Policy*, vol. 26, no. 65 (January 2011).

58. Auguste, Kihn, and Miller, *Closing the Talent Gap*.

59. Sam Dillon, "In Washington, Large Rewards in Teacher Pay," *New York Times*, December 31, 2011.

Chapter 3

1. The mystery is explicated thoroughly in Goldhaber, "The Mystery of Good Teaching," and most recently in Hanushek, "Higher Teacher Quality."

2. Suzanne Wilson, ed., *Teacher Quality*, Education Policy White Paper (Washington, DC: National Academy of Education, November 12, 2009).

3. See especially, Barber and Mourshed, *World's Best Performing School Systems*; Auguste, Kihn, and Miller, *Closing the Talent Gap*; and Tucker, *Standing on the Shoulders of Giants*.

4. See Decker, Mayer, and Glazerman, *Effects of Teach for America*; and Daniel Weisberg, Susan Sexton, Jennifer Mulhern, and David Keeling, *The Widget Effect: Our National Failure to Acknowledge and Act on Differences in Teacher Effectiveness* (Brooklyn, NY: The New Teacher Project, 2009).

5. The best overview of the administration's plans is found in *A Blueprint for Reform: The Reauthorization of the Elementary and Secondary Education Act* (Washington, DC: U.S. Department of Education, March 2010). A thoughtful

critique of the waiver strategy is offered by Martha Derthick and Andy Rotherham, "Obama's NCLB Waivers: Are They Necessary or Illegal?" *Education Next*, vol. 12, no. 2 (Spring 2012).

6. Moe and Chubb, *Liberating Learning*, chap. 5.

7. For example, see Thomas Kaplan and Kate Taylor, "Invoking King, Cuomo and Bloomberg Stoke Fight on Teacher Review Impasse," *New York Times,* January 16, 2012.

8. For one of the earliest studies, see Eric A. Hanushek, "Teacher Characteristics and Gains in Student Achievement: Estimation Using Micro-Data," *American Economic Review*, vol. 61, no. 2 (May 1971), pp. 280–88.

9. William L. Sanders and June C. Rivers, *Cumulative and Residual Effects of Teachers on Future Student Academic Achievement* (Knoxville, TN: University of Tennessee Value-Added Research and Assessment Center, 1996).

10. More conservative estimates of teacher effects are found in Barbara Nye, Spyros Konstantopoulos, and Larry V. Hedges, "How Large Are Teacher Effects?" *Educational Evaluation and Policy Analysis*, vol. 26, no. 3 (Fall 2004), pp. 237–57.

11. Effects were on the order of one-third of a standard deviation difference between top quartile and bottom quartile teachers. On New York, see Kane, Rockoff, and Staiger, "What Does Teacher Certification Tell Us?"; on Los Angeles, see Robert Gordon, Thomas Kane, and Douglas O. Staiger, *Identifying Teacher Performance on the Job* (Washington, DC: The Brookings Institution, 2006).

12. Raj Chetty, John N. Friedman, and Jonah E. Rockoff, "The Long-Term Impacts of Teachers: Teacher Value-Added and Student Outcomes in Adulthood," NBER Working Paper Series, Working Paper 17699 (Cambridge, MA: National Bureau of Economic Research, December 2011); and Annie Lowery, "Big Study Links Good Teachers to Lasting Gain," *New York Times*, January 6, 2012.

13. Eric A. Hanushek and Steven G. Rivkin, "Generalizing About Using Value-Added Measures of Teacher Quality," *American Economic Review*, vol. 100, no. 2 (May 2010), pp. 267–71.

14. Hanushek, "Economic Value." Effect sizes measure the change in student achievement in standard deviations associated with a one standard deviation difference in teacher quality. Hanushek places the average effect size for teachers across schools at 0.2 to 0.3, higher in math and lower in

reading. The difference in predicted achievement for teachers in the top and bottom quartile (about two standard deviations apart in effectiveness) translates into a year's worth of learning for one year of instruction.

15. Hassel and Ayscue Hassel, *Opportunity at the Top*.

16. See Eric A. Hanushek, "Teacher Deselection," in *Creating a New Teacher Profession*, eds. Goldhaber and Hannaway, chap. 8.

17. *Digest of Education Statistics*, table 285.

18. The number of master's degrees issued in education from 1990–91 to 2008–2009 more than doubled, while the number of teachers employed in public education increased by only one-third—an indication of the financial incentive to acquire a master's degree. *Digest of Education Statistics*, tables 68 and 285.

19. See Eric A. Hanushek and Steven G. Rivkin, "How to Improve the Supply of High Quality Teachers," in *Brookings Papers on Education Policy: 2004*, ed. Diane Ravitch (Washington, DC: The Brookings Institution Press, 2004), pp. 7–25.

20. Among many studies, see especially Donald Boyd, Pamela Grossman, Hamilton Lankford, Susanna Loeb, and James Wyckoff, "How Changes in Entry Requirements Alter the Teacher Workforce and Affect Student Achievement," *Education Finance and Policy*, vol. 1, no. 2 (Spring 2006), pp. 176–216; and Kane, Rockoff, and Staiger, "What Does Teacher Certification Tell Us?"

21. The difficulty of selecting promising teachers from resumes is highlighted in Jonah E. Rockoff, Brian A. Jacob, Thomas J. Kane, and Douglas O. Staiger, "Can You Recognize an Effective Teacher When You Recruit One?" NBER Working Paper Series, Working Paper 14485 (Cambridge, MA: National Bureau of Economic Research, November 2008).

22. Stephen Sawchuk, "Teacher Quality, Status Entwined Among Top-Performing Nations," *Education Week*, January 12, 2012.

23. Baccalaureate colleges focus mainly on liberal arts education for undergraduates and devote little resources to research. Master's universities top out with master's degrees, feature a mix of academic and professional programs, and are home to some research. Doctoral universities offer degrees from a bachelor of arts or science through PhD, cover many professional as well as academic fields, and emphasize research. Within each of these categories there are two sub-categories, distinguishing institutions that are more focused on a few fields from those that cover the gamut. See *The Carnegie Classification of Institutions of Higher Education*, Carnegie

Foundation for the Advancement of Teaching, http://classifications.carnegie foundation.org. Percentages of degrees are from Levine, *Educating School Teachers*, pp. 11–22.

24. For SAT and GPA averages and discussion, see Levine, *Educating School Teachers,* p. 72.

25. On faculty, ibid., pp. 73–75.

26. Ibid., pp. 76–79, 117–21. These results were obtained from a national sample of schools with wide variation in school quality. The selectivity of training institutions has been examined in other studies, with mixed results. Corroborating the findings of NWEA measures is Charles T. Clotfelter, Helen F. Ladd, and Jacob L. Vigdor, "Teacher Credentials and Student Achievement in High School: A Cross-Subject Analysis with Student Fixed Effects" (Washington, DC: CALDER [National Center for Analysis of Longitudinal Data in Education Research] Working Paper 11, 2007). A recent state study of Florida did not find that the quality of the college or university affected teacher success. See Matthew M. Chingos and Paul E. Peterson, "It's Easier to Pick a Good Teacher than to Train One: Familiar and New Results on the Correlates of Teacher Effectiveness," *Economics of Education Review,* vol. 30, no. 3 (June 2011), pp. 449–65.

27. *U.S. News & World Report,* "U.S. News College Compass: Best Colleges 2012," http://colleges.usnews.rankingsandreviews.com/best-colleges/rankings/national-universities.

28. Ibid.

29. Tennessee Higher Education Commission, *Report Card on the Effectiveness of Teacher Training Programs* (Nashville, TN: State Board of Education, December 1, 2010). Peabody produced statistically significant effects in math, as measured by comparisons with veteran teachers and with top quintile expectations. Teach for America produced statistically significant effects in math, science, and social studies. Sample sizes were smaller for Peabody because its graduates go on to teach in many states, leaving only about a dozen teaching grades three through eight core subjects each year. The TFA sample was larger. Both programs had t-statistics above state averages and above other teacher preparation programs, regardless of statistical significance.

30. Peabody scores from records supplied by the college. TFA data from Teach for America, http://www.teachforamerica.org.

31. Tennessee Higher Education Commission, *Report Card.*

32. Douglas O. Staiger and Jonah E. Rockoff, "Searching for Effective Teachers with Imperfect Information," *Journal of Economic Perspectives*, vol. 24, no. 3 (Summer 2010), pp. 97–118.

33. *National Assessment of Educational Progress, 2011 Mathematics and Reading Results by State*, Washington, DC: Institute of Education Sciences, National Center for Education Statistics, U.S. Department of Education.

34. Decker, Mayer, and Glazerman, *Effects of Teach for America*; Zeyu Xu, Jane Hannaway, and Colin Taylor, *Making a Difference? The Effects of Teach for America in High School* (Washington, DC: the Urban Institute and CALDER, March 2009); Jason A. Schoeneberger, Kelly A. Dever, and Lynne Tingle, *Evaluation of Teach for America in Charlotte-Mecklenburg Schools* (Charlotte, NC: Center for Research & Evaluation, Office of Accountability, Charlotte-Mecklenburg Schools, August 15, 2009).

35. Linda Darling-Hammond, Deborah J. Holtzman, Su Jin Gatlin, and Julian Vasquez Heilig, "Does Teacher Preparation Matter? Evidence About Teacher Certification, Teach for America, and Teacher Effectiveness," *Education Policy Analysis Archives,* vol. 13 (2005), pp. 1–47.

36. Morgaen L. Donaldson and Susan Moore Johnson, "The Price of Misassignment: The Role of Teaching Assignments in Teach for America Teachers' Exit from Low-Income Schools and the Teaching Profession," *Educational Evaluation and Policy Analysis*, vol. 32, no. 2 (June 2010), pp. 299–323.

37. All statistics from *U.S. News & World Report,* http://colleges.usnews.rankingsandreviews.com/best-colleges/rankings/national-universities.

38. Elizabeth D. Capaldi, John V. Lombardi, Craig W. Abbey, and Diane D. Craig, *The Top American Research Universities: 2010 Annual Report* (Arizona State University: The Center for Measuring University Performance, 2010).

39. "Best Graduate Schools," *U.S. News & World Report*, http://grad-schools.usnews.rankingsandreviews.com/best-graduate-schools.

40. Figures provided by Dean Camilla Benbow.

41. See, for example William H. Schmidt, Richard Houang, and Leland S. Cogan, "Preparing Future Math Teachers," *Science*, vol. 332, no. 6035 (June 10, 2011).

42. See, for example, Staiger and Rockoff, "Searching for Effective Teachers."

43. States are beginning to increase required hours of student teaching for initial licensure. As yet, there is not hard evidence that more student

teaching makes for more effective first-year teachers. At the same time, research into student teaching has not been able to control for the quality of the experience, just the quantity. The National Council on Teacher Quality has developed standards for quality student teaching experiences based on the available evidence—standards that Peabody more than satisfies. See Greenberg, Pomerance, and Walsh, *Student Teaching in the United States*, for those standards.

44. The National Council on Teacher Quality finds most teacher preparation programs do an inadequate job of ensuring that student teaching experiences are of high value to student teachers. See Greenberg, Pomerance, and Walsh, *Student Teaching in the United States*.

45. Yet, Peabody is not a boutique. Its highly selective master's program raises the school's annual teacher graduates to about 150 in all.

46. Special education majors are an exception, not requiring a second major.

47. For a survey of evidence, see Goldhaber, "The Mystery of Good Teaching."

48. See *Teacher Performance Assessment*, Stanford Center for Assessment, Learning, & Equity.

49. Levine, *Educating School Teachers*, pp. 31–33.

Chapter 4

1. In formal theories of organization the management problem is conceptualized as a principal-agent relationship, where the productivity of individual agents is difficult to measure and agents have disproportionately more information about their work than the principal. The solution lies in careful monitoring by the principal tempered by alignment of incentives of agents and the organization. For the classic treatment, see Oliver Williamson, *Markets and Hierarchies: Analysis and Antitrust Implications* (New York: The Free Press, 1975).

2. See Jim Collins, *Good to Great: Why Some Companies Make the Leap . . . and Others Don't* (New York: Harper Business, 2001).

3. Reporting on KIPP is based on an interview with the CEO of the KIPP Foundation, Richard Barth, and Director of Public Affairs Steve Mancini on November 22, 2011, as well as internal KIPP documents provided to me by the foundation. Those include KIPP Foundation, *Success as the Norm: Scaling up KIPP's Successful Leadership Development Model*, proposal to the U.S.

Department of Education, Investing in Innovation Grant Program, 2010; KIPP Foundation, *Leadership Design Academy*, 2011; and KIPP Foundation, "Leadership Competency Model," *Success as the Norm*, Appendix H.2.

4. See especially Katrina R. Woodworth, Jane L. David, Roneeta Guha, Haiwen Wang, and Alejandra Lopez-Torkos, *San Francisco Bay Area KIPP Schools: A Study of Early Implementation and Achievement, Final Report* (Menlo Park, CA: Center for Education Policy, SRI International, 2008); Aaron J. McDonald, Steven M. Ross, Jane Abney, and Todd Zoblotsky, *Urban School Reform: Year 4 Outcomes for the Knowledge is Power Program in an Urban Middle School*, paper presented at the annual meeting of the American Educational Research Association, March 2008; Martha A. Mac Iver and Elizabeth Farley-Ripple, *The Baltimore KIPP Ujima Village Academy, 2002–2006: A Longitudinal Analysis of Student Outcomes* (Baltimore: The Center for Social Organization of Schools, Johns Hopkins University, June 2007); and Educational Policy Institute, *Focus on Results: An Academic Impact Analysis of the Knowledge is Power Program* (Virginia Beach, VA, August 2005). A summary of studies is provided in Jeffrey R. Henig, "What Do We Know about the Outcomes at KIPP Schools?" (East Lansing, MI: Great Lakes Center for Education Research and Practice, November 2008).

5. On the differences in experimental and non-experimental approaches to the estimation of charter school effects, see Caroline M. Hoxby, Sonali Murarka, and Jenny Kang, *How New York City's Charter Schools Affect Student Achievement: August 2009 Report*, second report in series (Cambridge, MA: New York City Charter Schools Evaluation Project, September 2009); Thomas D. Cook, William R. Shadish, and Vivian C. Wong, "Three Conditions under Which Experiments and Observational Studies Produce Comparable Causal Estimates: New Findings from Within-Study Comparisons," *Journal of Policy Analysis and Management*, vol. 27, no. 4 (Autumn 2008), pp. 724–50.

6. Howard S. Bloom, Carolyn J. Hill, Alison Rebeck Black, and Mark W. Lipsey, *Performance Trajectories and Performance Gaps as Achievement Effect-Size Benchmarks for Educational Interventions*, MDRC Working Papers on Research Methodology, October 2008.

7. Jay Mathews, *Work Hard. Be Nice: How Two Inspired Teachers Created the Most Promising Schools in America* (Chapel Hill, NC: Algonquin Books, 2009).

8. See especially, KIPP Foundation, *Leadership Competency Model*.

9. Sir Michael Barber, Fenton Whelan, and Michael Clark, *Capturing the Leadership Premium: How the World's Top School Systems are Building Leadership Capacity for the Future* (New York: McKinsey & Company, 2010).

10. A recent exception is the New York City leadership development program. See Barber, Whelan, and Clark, *Capturing the Leadership Premium,* for a comparative analysis of it and programs from five other nations.

11. For a summary of the insights from "effective schools" research, see Stewart C. Purkey and Marshall S. Smith, "Effective Schools: A Review," *Elementary School Journal,* vol. 83, no. 4 (March 1983), pp. 427–52.

12. Barber, Whelan, and Clark, *Capturing the Leadership Premium,* p. 6, quoting from Kenneth Leithwood, Chistopher Day, Pam Sammons, Alma Harris, and David Hopkins, *Seven Strong Claims about Successful School Leadership,* 2006.

13. Tim Waters, Robert J. Marzano, and Brain McNulty, *Balanced Leadership: What 30 Years of Research Tells Us About the Effect of Leadership on Student Achievement* (Aurora, CO: Mid-continent Research for Education and Learning, 2003).

14. Frederick M. Hess, *Cage-Busting Leadership* (Cambridge, MA: Harvard Education Press, forthcoming).

15. Most recently, see Gregory F. Branch, Eric A. Hanushek, and Steven G. Rivkin, *Estimating the Effect of Leaders on Public Sector Productivity: The Case of School Principals,* NBER Working Paper 17803 (Cambridge, MA: National Bureau of Education Research, February 2012).

16. Ibid., pp. 23–25.

17. Alliance for Excellent Education, *What Keeps Good Teachers in the Classroom? Understanding and Reducing Teacher Turnover,* Issue Brief (Washington, DC: February, 2008); Richard M. Ingersoll, *Teacher Turnover, Teacher Shortages, and the Organization of Schools* (Seattle, WA: Center for the Study of Teaching and Policy, University of Washington, January 2001).

18. Martha Naomi Alt and Robin R. Henke, *To Teach or Not to Teach? Teaching Experience and Preparation Among 1992–93 Bachelor's Degree Recipients 10 Years After College* (Washington, DC: Institute of Educational Sciences, National Center for Education Statistics, U.S. Department of Education, July 2007).

19. Eric A. Hanushek, John F. Kain, and Steven G. Rivkin, "Why Public Schools Lose Teachers," *Journal of Human Resources,* vol. 39, no. 2 (Spring 2004), pp. 326–54; and Eric A. Hanushek and Steven G. Rivkin,

"Pay, Working Conditions, and Teacher Quality," *The Future of Children*, vol. 17, no. 1 (Spring 2007), pp. 69–86.

20. Brian Jacob and Lars Lefgren, "When Principals Rate Teachers: The Best—and The Worst—Stand Out," *Education Next*, vol. 6, no. 2 (Spring 2006), pp. 59–64.

21. Thomas J. Kane and Douglas O. Staiger, *Gathering Feedback for Teaching: Combining High-Quality Observations with Student Surveys and Achievement Gains*, MET Project, Policy and Practice Brief, Bill & Melinda Gates Foundation, January 2010.

22. Hillsborough County, a large school district in Florida, has pioneered this practice since 2009 with a $100 million grant from the Gates Foundation.

23. Rockoff, Jacob, Kane, and Staiger, "Can You Recognize an Effective Teacher?"

24. On experience, see Hanushek and Rivkin, "Teacher Quality."

25. See, for example, Michael S. Garet, Andrew J. Wayne, Fran Stancavage, James Taylor, Kirk Walters, Mengli Song, Seth Brown, and Steven Hurlburt, *Middle School Mathematics Professional Development Impact Study: Findings After the First Year of Implementation* (Washington, DC: Institute of Educational Sciences, National Center for Education Statistics, U.S. Department of Education, April 2010).

26. John E. Chubb and Terry M. Moe, *Politics, Markets, and America's Schools* (Washington, DC: The Brookings Institution, 1990).

27. Jenny Anderson, "States Try to Fix Quirks in Teacher Evaluations," *New York Times*, February 19, 2012.

28. *Digest of Education Statistics*, table 89.

Chapter 5

1. On this general theme, see especially Moe and Chubb, *Liberating Learning*, chap. 3.

2. *Digest of Education Statistics*, table 89.

3. The administration made value-added assessment a condition of all of its major initiatives, from "stimulus" funds provided by the American Recovery and Reinvestment Act, to the Race to the Top competitive grant competition, to the issuance of waivers from the requirements of No Child

Left Behind. The administration's enforcement of these conditions was uneven at best, leaving much room for improvement in the states.

4. The Obama administration made elimination of caps on charter schools a condition of the Race to the Top competition and a principle behind its other major initiatives, with uneven enforcement.

5. On the main obstacles and remedies, see Paul T. Hill, ed., *Charter Schools Against the Odds: An Assessment of the Koret Task Force on K–12 Education* (Stanford, CA: Hoover Institution Press, 2007).

6. For the strongest, most recent studies, see Hoxby, Murarka, and Kang, *New York City's Charter Schools*; and CREDO (Center for Research on Education Outcomes), *Multiple Choice: Charter School Performance in 16 States*, Stanford, CA: 2009.

7. Barber, Whelan, and Clark, *Capturing the Leadership Premium*.

8. See especially Barber, Whelan, and Clark, *Capturing the Leadership Premium*; and Tucker, *Standing on the Shoulders of Giants*.

9. The measurement and estimation of the added value of training programs presents non-trivial technical challenges that are still in the process of being solved. Of paramount importance is acquiring sufficient data points in sufficient numbers of schools to separate confidently the training effects from other effects on student achievement. States are currently experimenting with methods.

10. For a detailed outline of measures recommended to create a healthy market for education technology, see John E. Chubb, "Overcoming the Governance Challenge in K–12 Online Learning," in *Creating Sound Policy for Digital Learning*, working paper series (Washington, DC: Thomas B. Fordham Institute, February 16, 2012).

About the Author

John E. Chubb is the interim chief executive officer (CEO) of Education Sector, an independent education think tank in Washington, DC, a distinguished visiting fellow at the Hoover Institution at Stanford University, and a member of the Koret Task Force on K–12 Education at Hoover. He previously served as CEO of Leeds Global Partners and chief education officer of EdisonLearning, of which he was a founder. He has also been a senior fellow at the Brookings Institution and a faculty member at Stanford University. His books include *Liberating Learning: Technology, Politics and the Future of American Education*, with Terry M. Moe, *Learning from No Child Left Behind: How and Why the Nation's Most Important but Controversial Education Law Should Be Renewed, Bridging the Achievement Gap*, with Tom Loveless, and *Politics, Markets and America's Schools*, with Terry M. Moe.

KORET TASK FORCE ON K–12 EDUCATION

The Koret Task Force on K–12 Education is a top-rate team of education experts brought together by the Hoover Institution at Stanford University with the support of the Koret Foundation and other foundations and individuals, to work on education reform. The primary objectives of the task force are to gather, evaluate, and disseminate existing evidence in an analytical context, and analyze reform measures that will enhance the quality and productivity of K–12 education.

The Koret Task Force on K–12 Education includes some of the most highly regarded and best known education scholars in the nation. Most are professors at some of the leading universities in the country and many have served in various executive and advisory roles for federal, state, and local governments. Their combined expertise represents over 300 years of research and study in the field of education. Current members of the task force are John E. Chubb, Williamson M. Evers, Chester E. Finn Jr. (current chair), Eric A. Hanushek, Paul T. Hill, Caroline M. Hoxby, Tom Loveless, Terry M. Moe, Paul E. Peterson, Herbert J. Walberg, and Grover J. Whitehurst.

The eleven-member task force forms the centerpiece of the Hoover Institution's Initiative on American Educational Institutions and Academic Performance. In addition to producing original research, analysis, and recommendations in a growing body of work on the most important issues in American education today, task force members serve as editors, contributors, and members of the editorial board of *Education Next: A Journal of Opinion and Research*, published by the Hoover Institution. For further information, please see the task force website.

www.hoover.org/taskforces/education

Index

EDUCATION next BOOKS

EDUCATION NEXT BOOKS address major subjects related to efforts to reform American public education. This imprint features assessments and monographs by Hoover Institution fellows (including members of the Hoover Institution's Koret Task Force on K–12 Education), as well as those of outside experts.